TEACH

Creating Independently Responsible Learners

Dennis DiNoia, M.A.Ed

TEACH: Creating Independently Responsible Learners

https://mrdmath.com

Published by Made to Change the World™ Publishing
Nashville, Tennessee

ISBN: 978-1-956837-84-1 (paperback)
ISBN: 978-1-956837-85-8 (ebook)

Printed globally.

DEDICATION

To my students, past, present, and future, this book is for you. You've taught me that so much more becomes possible when a learner discovers their own brilliance. You've shown me that hardship can build confidence, that mistakes can create momentum for growth, and that learning can be a joyful adventure.

To the families I serve, who show up every day with a desire to help their young people thrive, you make this work matter.

Whoever you are, wherever you are on your journey, welcome. I see you. I believe in you.

May you find exactly what you need here.

TABLE OF CONTENTS

Foreword 1

Acknowledgments 5

Preface 7

Introduction 9

CHAPTER 1 - An Accidental Discovery 11

Dropout prevention classes 13

The sunday grading grind 13

The experiment 15

Remembering 8th-grade algebra 17

Gaps in the system 20

The first glimpse of the independently responsible learner 21

CHAPTER 2 - The Independently Responsible Learner 23

Defining "independently" and "responsible" 25

Why most curricula fail 27

Homeschooling 28

Multi-sensory lessons 30

Mistakes 32

From math skills to life skills 34

CHAPTER 3 - The Parent Is the Coach 37

Shifting roles 39

Signs of ownership and mastery 40

Questions instead of answers 41

The three common gaps 43

The coach–player analogy 44

Normalizing independently responsible learners 45

CHAPTER 4 - The Student Is the Teacher **47**
Why teaching is the pathway to mastery 49
Math as an example 50
The teach-back effect 52
A practical exercise 53
Bringing learning into their world 55

CHAPTER 5 - Checking Your Own Work **59**
Why most people were never trained to check their own work 61
Learning vs. Knowing 62
What goes wrong 63
Mistakes 65

CHAPTER 6 - Present Yourself **67**
What this really means 69
Flow state 70
Multiple intelligences 71
Creative formats 73
Presentations as preparation 74
A personal assignment 75

CHAPTER 7 - Testing, Testing, 1-2-3 . . . . **77**
Tests in school and in life 79
Secret #1 81
Secret #2 82
Secret #3 89

CHAPTER 8 - Learning How to Think **91**
Traditional learning trains memorizing, not thinking 93
Discovering your learning style 94

Learning questions 95

Using your learning style 98

How learning styles support independently responsible learning 100

Knowing how you think 101

CHAPTER 9 – Do What You Love to Do 103

Interviews with successful people 105

Personal story 106

“If you do what you love, the money will find you” 108

Goals 110

A 5-step process for discovering what you love 112

Doing what you love is a model for your children 115

CHAPTER 10 – Mastermind 117

What is a mastermind? 119

How to run a mastermind group 120

Keeping goals alive 123

BONUS CHAPTER – Goal-Setting 125

Redefining goals 127

Step 1 129

Step 2 131

Step 3 134

Sharing your story 135

A Note from Me to You 137

About the Author. 139

Praise for *Teach* 141

FOREWORD

There are educators who teach content, and there are educators who teach students. Then there are rare educators like Dennis DiNoia, who spark something deeper: genuine ownership of learning. Over the past seven years of collaborating with Dennis, I have watched his work consistently change how students see themselves and what they believe they can do. His approach reaches far beyond math. It builds confidence, resilience, and a sense of personal responsibility that carries into every subject and every stage of life.

I have been an educator for 26 years and a high school administrator for nearly ten of them. In that time, I have seen many instructional models, programs, and initiatives. Very few have impressed me the way Dennis's framework has. His work aligns with what I believe most deeply about education: students thrive when they understand that learning is something they can direct and shape, not something that happens to them.

My professional respect for Dennis became personal when my daughter enrolled in his pre-calculus course in high school. She entered the class with a mixture of uncertainty and determination, but what she found there changed her entire view of her own education. The structure of his course, the way he asks students to think and check their understanding, and the intentional transfer of responsibility into her own hands helped my daughter see herself differently. She not only completed the class but also grew into a student who trusted her own reasoning.

That shift carried her forward beyond Dennis's classroom. Today, she has completed her differential equations course at a California State University as part of her degree in data science. Watching her step into that advanced work with confidence reminded me of the lasting impact of the mindset she gained in Mr. D's course. It was not only preparation in skill; it was preparation in belief.

This book captures that philosophy with clarity. *Teach: Creating Independently Responsible Learners* is more than a guide. It is an invitation to transform how we support young people. In education, we often talk about developing agency, motivation, and student ownership, yet many approaches remain too abstract or too complex to sustain. Dennis offers something different. His strategies are practical, repeatable, and grounded in real classrooms and experiences.

Over the years, I have watched thousands of students respond to this approach. Learners who once doubted their abilities begin to trust their thinking. High-achieving students learn how to work through struggle rather than avoid it. Families notice a shift in how their children approach challenges. Educators rediscover what becomes possible when students are treated as active partners in their own learning.

This second edition arrives at a critical moment. Students today are entering a world that requires adaptability, problem-solving, and self-direction. Memorization and compliance will not carry them into that future. The habits of mind described in this book will.

Whether you are a classroom teacher, a parent, a school leader, or simply someone who cares deeply about helping young people grow, you will find both inspiration and actionable ideas in these pages. You will see how responsibility can be guided rather than forced, how independence can be nurtured, and how students can rise when given the structure and trust to do so.

As an educator, high school administrator, and parent, I have witnessed the impact of this approach firsthand. It shaped my daughter's path into advanced mathematics and data science. It has influenced my own leadership. And I believe it can open doors for countless other learners.

I am honored to introduce this edition of *Teach: Creating Independently Responsible Learners*. My hope is that as you read, you will discover not only new strategies but a renewed belief in what students are capable of when we trust them to take the lead.

Traci King
Educational Leader and High School Administrator

ACKNOWLEDGMENTS

I want to thank the students who first invited me to see learning through their eyes. You're the reason this book exists. The young people in those early classroom years, the homeschoolers who took a chance on a brand-new math program, and the countless students who asked honest questions challenged my thinking and taught me just as much as I ever taught them. You are the heartbeat behind the idea of the independently responsible learner.

My thanks to all the parents who, whether from kitchen tables, classrooms, or the other side of a computer screen, have partnered with me to make their child's learning more meaningful. Thank you for your trust, your courage, your honesty, and your commitment to helping your young people discover what they are truly capable of.

I am deeply grateful for the coaches, teachers, colleagues, and friends who encouraged me to think differently about education, and who kept reminding me that it was possible to build something new. To the "Mr. D Math Team" (many of whom began as students and families but are now part of this global community of educators), thank you for living these principles and bringing them to life for so many others.

I want to acknowledge my parents for all that they have done for me. While my father is now deceased, his dedication to being on the cutting edge as an educator gave me the courage to do the same. My mother, Gail DiNoia, has been my biggest cheerleader from the start. She has always been a "yes" to my new ideas. She assisted in editing this book and is one of the most amazing and inspiring women I know. I love you, Mom!

And to my family, you are amazing for all that you are and in all that you do. You have supported me through every late-night idea, recorded lesson, new course, and crazy, “What if we tried this?” Thank you for embracing the concepts of independently responsible learning as we have woven them into our own homeschool curriculum. Your love and belief in me imbue every chapter of this book.

PREFACE

As you read or listen to this book, search for the nuggets that speak directly to you, like you're mining for gold. Note what stands out as meaningful to you. This book was written from the perspective of the independently responsible learner. Throughout these pages, you will discover for yourself what that means, and you will discover it more than once. I hope you will use these discoveries to serve the students in your life and foster their journey toward becoming independently responsible learners. I hope your discoveries reawaken your curiosity and confidence as an educator, just as they did for me.

INTRODUCTION

Every so often in life, you stumble upon an idea that changes everything. Not all at once, but slowly, quietly, and then unmistakably. For me, that idea emerged in a classroom full of students who had already been told, in one way or another, that they weren't going to make it. They were labeled "at risk," "unmotivated," or "left behind." It was clear that the standard education system was failing them. So, as I stood before them at the front of a classroom, I had a powerful realization: They didn't need another teacher to throw information at them; they needed someone to show them how to think, discover, and take responsibility for their own learning.

This book is the story of that discovery and the journey that followed.

What began as an experiment within a dropout prevention program became the foundation for everything I have taught since. It led me to an entirely new understanding of learning, one that teaches young people to step into confidence, ownership, and self-direction. It led to the creation of an educational method now used by thousands of families worldwide. And most importantly, it led me to one unmistakable truth:

When a student takes responsibility for their learning, everything becomes possible.

This book is not about fixing children. It is not about forcing them to work harder or learn faster. It is about awakening something that already exists inside each of them: The curiosity, capability, and confidence that too often get buried under memorization, instruction-heavy teaching, and a fear of making mistakes.

Within these pages, you'll discover how to create the optimal conditions for a young person to become an independently responsible learner. You will see the power in having students check their own work, present their own thinking, and teach what they have learned. You'll also come to understand the importance of shifting your own role from that of a teacher to that of a coach. You'll learn how this method transforms not only a student's grades, but also their personal responsibility, communication, resilience, self-belief, and entire future. And you will see that when a learner becomes a teacher, their education becomes more profound, more meaningful, and more joyful.

Whether you are a parent, teacher, mentor, or young person reading this for yourself, this book is an invitation. I invite you to think differently about learning, to challenge old assumptions, and to step into a future where young people are confident thinkers, problem-solvers, creators, and doers. As you read, you may begin to notice something surprising: This journey is not just about the student—It is also about the educator. Becoming a coach, a guide, or a partner in learning will require as much growth from you as becoming an independently responsible learner will from your learner.

As you read, you'll come to see what I've seen over the past several decades: That students are far more capable than we give them credit for, that learning is far more natural than we make it, and that when we give young people the tools to discover knowledge for themselves, they rise higher than any curriculum alone could ever take them.

Chapter 1

AN ACCIDENTAL DISCOVERY

DROPOUT PREVENTION CLASSES

I will never forget the moment I realized that something was broken in the education system.

I started my teaching career in 1988 as a math teacher working with a group of struggling students—young people enrolled in what was referred to as the "dropout prevention" program. The program was designed to be their last chance to succeed in school and get an education. Our students hadn't been successful in previous schools, and if they didn't make it in our program, they would likely be done with school altogether.

The dropout rate hung around 30%, and most of the students felt frustrated and hopeless about their future prospects. Many of them didn't want to be there and faced challenges outside the classroom: divorced parents, unsafe neighborhoods, drug and alcohol addictions, limited access to food, and an overall lack of motivation. These students had to navigate debilitating situations before they even made it to the classroom every morning.

Did all my students have to endure these difficulties? No, but many did. I knew that for them, my math class wouldn't be a top priority. Was I going to make math fun and exciting enough to change this? Probably not. But was there a way I could try to make learning math more meaningful to them, something they had never seen or experienced before, something they could take pride in? All I knew was that I was determined to try.

THE SUNDAY GRADING GRIND

I began by asking myself: "What would make a difference in the lives of these young people? What needs to change to get them on the right track?" As I went to work on answering these questions, I discovered a secret along the way.

I started by doing what I thought any good teacher would do. I wanted my students to turn in their assignments and homework so I could grade them. I thought that if I could take a look at what they were doing well and what they were struggling with, make corrections, and give them detailed feedback, then perhaps I could build relationships with them and get them more engaged in the classroom. I was naive enough to believe that if I could just get my students to do their homework, everything else would fall into place! I thought that if they could see their mistakes, they would begin to learn from them, and it would open their eyes to their own potential. I thought that by putting my time and attention into assessing their work, it would show them that someone actually cared and believed in them.

So, every week, the students would turn in their work, and I would tell them, "Okay, I am going to take all of your work home over the weekend. I am going to grade it and give you notes so that you can understand where you went wrong. Then, I am going to try to help you understand how to correct your mistakes."

That is where it all began. Every Sunday, I sat down and spent the *entire* day grading assignments. I didn't have that many students (150 in total), but I wrote extensive notes on every page, giving them different suggestions and illustrating how to do the work properly. I told myself I would do whatever it took to show them a path to success. I was sure that they were capable of achieving so much more if they could simply understand their mistakes.

You have to understand that this was my first year of teaching. I was overly excited, and I wanted to make a difference. I was sure that if I could just connect with my students, something would click, and it would keep them in school and on the right track. I wanted them to believe there could be more to their lives—that they were each worthy of a better life than the one they had. I wanted them to graduate and maybe even go to college. But when I handed back their carefully marked homework, rather than suddenly realizing the full scope of their academic potential, my students glanced at their grades, glanced back up at me, and just put their papers away without reviewing a single problem. This continued week after week—they all did the same thing. Nobody even bothered to look at their homework or read all my amazing Sunday feedback! More importantly, nobody was interested in building a rapport.

This went on for the entirety of that first semester of my teaching career. Every weekend, without exception, I wrote my Sunday feedback. I graded papers and sacrificed something that was very important to me: football! Back in 1988, we couldn't watch replays of the game, so if I missed the play, I missed the play. That was tough, especially once I started to realize that the students didn't seem to care about the feedback or my efforts anyway.

I started to feel frustrated. I was trying so hard, but nothing seemed to be changing. It felt like there was nothing I could do to make a difference for these students. By the end of the semester, I knew that something had to give.

THE EXPERIMENT

The apparent failure of my Sunday Feedback to get through to my students led me to try a new experiment. I wasn't sure it would work, but I had to try something different. I felt that I was on the verge of giving up on them—after all, it seemed like they had already given up on themselves—and that wasn't the type of teacher I wanted to be. And if I'm really honest with myself, I was just frustrated that no matter how much work I put in, they didn't seem interested in meeting me halfway.

I started to reconsider my teaching methods. I wondered if maybe it was my approach, rather than the students, that needed to change. I had been trying to control something that was out of my control—my students' interest in the material. So, I decided to redirect my energy towards what I could control. When the second semester began, I started my classes by telling the students that we were going to do things differently from then on. I wasn't going to grade their work anymore—I wanted them to grade it themselves. Sometimes, I wonder if this idea arose from my frustration at all of the Sunday Football games I had missed, but it actually came to me as I started looking for out-of-the-box ways to get the students engaged without making my own workload unmanageable. What if there was a way for them to take ownership—responsibility—of their work by inner choice, rather than external assignment?

I knew that all the answers to their homework problems were in the back of their textbooks, so I asked the students to do their homework as usual, but then they were to check their own work using the textbook answers and bring me their grades the next day. But there was a catch: They also had to tell me the percentage they'd gotten on each assignment. So, right from the start, they had to develop a new math skill in order to calculate their score. It wasn't just about the homework; it was about getting them curious about learning. I was asking them to go beyond what was expected of them and challenging them to think critically about what they were doing.

Sure enough, the students started doing their homework and checking it on their own. From there, they soon started to see what they were getting wrong. This sparked a natural curiosity in them. They started asking questions about the answers they had gotten wrong. They had been given the solutions, but not the steps to get there on their own. Now, when they weren't getting good grades, they wanted to know why. Suddenly, they were interested. Sometimes they would even argue that the textbook was wrong and their answer was correct! They started teaching themselves to find the solutions themselves before marking, by looking at examples in the book or their own notes from class.

When I'd graded their work in the past, I'd told them what was wrong with their answers, but they never asked any questions. They only looked at the grades. Now they were grading their own work, and all of a sudden, they were curious. They were learning, and more importantly, they were taking responsibility for their education.

This whole experiment operated on an honor system, if you will. Allowing students to grade their own assignments naturally created a temptation, in some, to stretch the truth in their own favor. In addition to making students responsible for their own integrity, I implemented a system to confirm that they were actually doing the work as they claimed. While they graded their homework, I wrote and graded the unit quizzes and exams myself. When I graded their exams, I could point out to a student who claimed to earn 100 percent on every homework assignment but failed the test that something wasn't adding up. I could work with that student to try to understand the disparity in their homework and test scores. Usually, it came down to a lack of integrity! They hadn't actually been doing the work they claimed. But the interesting thing I started to notice was that, on average, my students' test scores were higher in the second semester, when they were responsible for grading their own homework, than in the first, when I graded everything myself. And on top of all of that, I had gotten my Sundays back! I realized I was finally seeing the outcomes I had been hoping for all along, so I kept going.

REMEMBERING 8TH-GRADE ALGEBRA

While I watched the students grow over the course of the semester, I remembered an experience from my own time at school.

In 1975, I was in the eighth grade, and I was far from a model student. I was a musician—a trumpet player—and I still am to this day. When I was in school, I would neglect my academics to practice for hours every day. Outside of school, I also played baseball, was socially involved, and wanted a girlfriend—as many kids that age do! Then, at the bottom of this list of priorities, there was also this thing called homework. I would try to complete as much work as possible in class, but it wasn't a priority. My music, sport, and social life left little time for homework. My grades weren't bad, and I was getting mostly B's, but I wasn't reaching my full potential.

Apparently, I had an aptitude for math, so despite my delinquency, I was placed in the Advanced Algebra 1 class. But there was still this little problem of finding time for homework. My teacher in that class had a solution manual for the textbook, and he always let us use it to check our work if we wanted to understand the explanations better.

One day, he gave us a test and allowed us to use our homework to complete it. I hadn't done the homework properly, but then I remembered the solution manual. I asked the teacher if I could use it for the test, and he said yes.

During the test, whenever a question stumped me, I would find a similar question in the solution manual, and then figure out how it had been solved. Then I would apply those steps to the test question. I realized that I was learning as I took the test—and I was teaching myself. I got the highest grade in the class on that test! But the real victory for me was the discovery that I was in charge of my learning—that I could grow if I wanted to. I didn't have to wait for someone or something else to make it happen.

If I could see how something had been solved, I could figure it out. And if I could figure it out, I could learn anything. In that moment, my confidence in myself exploded. My own journey to becoming an independently responsible learner had begun.

This is the foundation of everything I now believe about learning: Students don't need someone to do the thinking for them. What they really need is someone to show them how to discover the answers for themselves. That insight became the core of my relationship with teaching and learning long before I even thought about becoming a teacher myself.

And with my new confidence, the world suddenly looked very different. Fast forward to my classroom in 1988 again, and my students were starting to take an interest in what they were doing. They were asking questions, their grades were improving, but more importantly, their relationship to learning was changing. They were starting to take ownership of their own work. Many years later, at their 25-year high school reunion, I met some of my students from that 1988 class who had been told that they would never make it. My dropout prevention program alumni had gone on to become entrepreneurs and professionals living successful and meaningful lives.

I was so proud of the people they had become, and they were excited to see me, too. This was due to the bond we had built during my time as their math teacher. I had given them the opportunity to discover their own potential by finding solutions for themselves, and that had a lasting effect on them. One student contacted me 30 years after I had been his teacher to tell me how much my class had made a difference in his life. When I first met him, he was on the verge of dropping out of high school. When I spoke to him decades later as an adult, he had become an entrepreneur, operating a business building custom audio solutions for his clients in their homes and offices. From the start, it was clear that my experiment in creating independently responsible learners was creating positive outcomes in the classroom, but I couldn't have predicted how much it would impact my students' lives in the long term. Today, I can see the results, and it has shaped everything I have done in my teaching career, from my work as a public school teacher to creating my own curriculum and establishing programs for the homeschooling community.

GAPS IN THE SYSTEM

In case you didn't know this, public school teachers don't make a lot of money, so like many of my fellow educators, I have often needed a second job over the course of my career. Many years after I'd first implemented this method in my classrooms, I got the chance to work as an after-school math tutor. Unlike teaching in a school, where I worked with only a narrow age range of students, while working as a tutor, I connected with students of all ages. I got to see them from first grade all the way up through the end of high school and into college. Working with such a wide range of students was very impactful because, as I taught, I also learned. I was learning math through the eyes of third-graders, sixth-graders, and eighth-graders. I got to see all of the different textbooks and curricula that were out there. I was hearing all the best instruction strategies used by all the best teachers. I became the ultimate student because I was exposed to all of it at once—I could see how math was taught to students from their first assignments in elementary school to their final standardized tests in preparation for undergraduate study.

I started looking for the connections between what a kid learned as a third-grader and what they would need to know by the time they became a sixth-grader. I could work with an eighth-grader and know what was coming for them once they entered high school. As a public school teacher, I'm usually limited to working with a particular grade or within a specific subject. A high school math teacher might teach an algebra or a geometry class, but they wouldn't be able to see where the students were coming from, or where they were when they entered middle or elementary school. I had noticed that there were gaps in the knowledge of the students entering my own high school classroom, but I didn't know where those gaps had come from until I started tutoring multiple age groups.

Tutoring allowed me to see where those gaps were coming from and try to find ways to bridge them. I was able to see what the future was going to be like for students and what they would need to succeed. I saw the gaps between what students learned in elementary school and what they would need to know as they entered middle school. This allowed me to fill in the blanks for my elementary school-aged students to make sure they were well prepared, rather than having to play catch-up, once they got to middle school. My understanding of where my students were coming from and where they would be going allowed me to fill the frustrating gaps in knowledge created by the current education system. These issues don't only frustrate math teachers; they create problems for educators across all subject areas. If educators had a better understanding of what their students had learned in the past and what they would need to know in the future, it would smooth the transitions between grade levels.

THE FIRST GLIMPSE OF THE INDEPENDENTLY RESPONSIBLE LEARNER

I tutored as a second source of income for several years, and in the process, I became really great at teaching math to young people of all ages. As I said, I had learned so many different teaching strategies that I could find the one that fit best for each student. So, in trying to bridge the gap in my finances, I accidentally started bridging the gaps in the education system! I also noticed, again and again, that students were most successful when they were encouraged to do their own work and discover the answers for themselves. I made sure that students were telling me about what they were learning in all their subjects, not just math. These are the kinds of conversations that build relationships between teachers and students, and by teaching me what they were learning, they were making sense of it for themselves. They were mastering the material, rather than simply memorizing it. The students were experiencing what it is like to be an independently responsible learner. They were deepening their understanding of what they had learned by teaching it to someone else.

My conversations and questions with my students had also changed. "Walk me through this. How did you get that answer? Show me an example. Here is one all worked out. Show me how it's done and talk to me through each step. How does that apply to the problem you're working on?" More and more, I was teaching my students by asking them questions, rather than giving them lectures.

Not only were my students gaining confidence in their abilities, but they were also recognizing that the same process I had discovered as an eighth-grader still worked for them. They saw that they could check their own work, learn from examples, and even teach someone else by sharing their own understanding.

In the next chapter, we're going to take a deeper dive into what an independently responsible learner is and how a young person can become one.

Chapter 2

THE INDEPENDENTLY RESPONSIBLE LEARNER

DEFINING "INDEPENDENTLY" AND "RESPONSIBLE"

In this chapter, you're going to discover how independently responsible learning works in practice.

As my career advanced—first as a school teacher and then in the tutoring business—a point came when I knew I needed to develop my ideas into a program. As far as I could tell, the independently responsible learner mindset wasn't being fostered or developed in most learning environments. In public school classrooms—especially in math programs—this approach was not being encouraged. So I began to ask myself how I could create that kind of learner in my own classroom? But I knew that if I was going to try something nontraditional, I was going to have to step out of the traditional public school system.

So I did.

While continuing my work in the public school system, I started focusing on my true passion: working with homeschool students. Families who choose homeschooling do so for a number of different reasons, often relating to the behavioral, physical, or academic needs of their learners. Sometimes families choose homeschooling because the student is an athlete, musician, or artist and needs to devote more time to their specialty. Whatever the reason, all my students had one thing in common: They were young people who were ready to learn.

When I say "independently responsible learner," I mean a student who has taken ownership of their own learning. Let's analyze each word- "independently" and "responsible"—and then put them together to come up with a working definition.

When I say independently, I mean acting in a way that is free from outside control or influence. This means you are acting in a manner of complete freedom. And what does it mean to be responsible? To be responsible is to have a job or duty. A responsible person is trusted to do what is right, expected, or required of them. Those are the definitions of the two parts. Now let's put them together.

Being independently responsible means being trusted to do things independently in the way they are meant to be done. Simply put, an independently responsible learner doesn't have anyone telling them what to do or how to do it, but that doesn't mean they can't ask for help. Being independently responsible also means having the freedom and willingness to ask for support when it is needed.

Parents can partner with their children to help them become independently responsible learners. Many parents already teach responsibility in other areas of life, like chores, friendships, and jobs. Doesn't it make sense to take the same approach with education? Employers also want this in their employees. People who take initiative, follow through, and can be trusted to own their work make for a great workforce. When students learn to be independently responsible, it allows them to thrive academically now and professionally in the future.

Think about a child's day. School and learning occupy so many of their waking hours. If a student doesn't learn how to take responsibility for their learning, they can develop habits of dependence that parents end up having to address at home. But when students learn to take ownership of their learning at school, everything else changes as well. They start thinking for themselves, noticing their own patterns, taking responsibility for getting their work done, making wise decisions, and discovering that they are capable.

So, an independently responsible learner is someone who takes ownership of their own learning process. They know how to get the information they need, how to use examples to figure things out for themselves, and how to draw their own conclusions before running to someone else for the answer. They know when to seek help, but they don't rely on it as their first step. They approach learning with curiosity and initiative rather than waiting to be told what to do.

This doesn't mean that students should be left alone without direction. It means we, as educators, should teach them how to think, not just what to think. Instead of doing the work for them, we should give them the tools and examples they need to do the work themselves. Guidance isn't taken away—it's transformed into a form of support that gives the learner responsibility for their own education. This led me to a new question: How do I structure my math course—or any course—to transform my students into independently responsible learners?

WHY MOST CURRICULA FAIL

I immediately started experimenting with ways to encourage students to take initiative and be resourceful rather than depending on others to do the work for them. My goal wasn't to withhold support but to create learning experiences that invited students to watch, observe, notice, test, and discover things for themselves. When students could study a finished example and figure out why it worked, they would start understanding the math behind it on a deeper level. They weren't just memorizing procedures; they were making sense of them. At the same time, I kept noticing something missing from the textbooks my students used. No matter what book I opened, none of them trained students to take responsibility for their own learning. Everything was laid out in a way that encouraged them to follow instructions rather than develop their own understanding of the material.

That realization pushed me to think differently. What would a curriculum look like if its core purpose were to develop independently responsible learners? How could I create a program that helped students discover math for themselves, while still giving them the support they needed along the way? The answer began forming through my work as a tutor. As I modeled independent responsibility to my students, they started to embody it themselves. I started coaching parents on how to support the transformations they were seeing in their learners at home as well as school, and the results were quick and powerful.

HOMESCHOOLING

One day, a mother I had been working with said, “Mr. D, why don’t you write your own curriculum?” I had thought about it for years, but doubted whether I could pull it off. I knew I could write lessons and create practice problems, but for a full curriculum, I would need to include instructional videos, and that felt like a huge hurdle.

But my mind latched on to the possibility until one day I found out about a new recording software that made it all possible. Suddenly, I had the tools I needed to create my program, so I taught myself how to record, edit, and produce video lessons. I became a student again, going step by step exactly the way I wanted my students to learn! I was practicing the very thing I was teaching: becoming an independently responsible learner. And seeing that I could learn this way cemented my belief that the method was applicable to any student, no matter the learner or the subject matter.

I reflected on my own eighth-grade experience again. If seeing how problems were solved helped me figure things out, what if my students could watch me solve example problems on command? What if they could hear it, see it, and interact with it all at the same time? With this in mind, I began looking for ways to bring my method to life. I started developing video lessons that trained students to explore and discover learning for themselves.

Each video lesson I produced contained instructions and examples. The lessons were also accompanied by practice problems and a detailed solution manual, which went far beyond the answers found at the back of standard textbooks.

While recording the videos, I became concerned about the attention spans of my potential students. I turned to two sources of inspiration. First, there was a teaching method I had learned years earlier called *Super Teach,* which uses colors to attract and engage students' attention. Second, there was the theory of conditioning attention employed by advertisements on television. It's not a common occurrence in today's world anymore because people don't watch television commercials as much as they used to, but when television was developed, you would watch a show for approximately seven minutes, and then there would be a 30, 60, or 90-second commercial break.

Our attention spans were conditioned by television to be seven minutes long. These days, social media and short-form videos are shrinking attention spans even further! In my videos, I needed to make sure I could continuously regain a student's attention so they could stay engaged through the entire lesson. I decided that every few moments, I would change the color of the writing on the screen. By changing the colors of the writing on the screen, I could recapture my students' attention and reorient them back to the content over and over again. Each time the colors changed, their attention span was reset. My hope was that, over time, this methodology would help increase the attention spans of my students and keep them focused on the course material.

MULTI-SENSORY LESSONS

Many people don't know that there are many different types of learning. Auditory learners are most successful when they are taught through conversation and description, visual learners prefer diagrams and images, and tactile learners prefer to learn in ways that let them get their hands around the problem. My videos supported all learning styles by giving students different ways to connect with the material. For visual learners, lessons were presented with visible examples that unfolded one piece at a time. For auditory learners, I made sure to explain the reasoning behind each step in solving a problem, providing the explanations in a conversational and easy-to-follow format. For tactile learners, I provided plenty of practice problems for them to work through at their own pace, and provided examples for them to examine and figure out for themselves, as opposed to simply memorizing a set of equations. And for those who preferred reading and writing, I provided written guides, practice tests, and opportunities to express mathematical concepts in their own words.

Most importantly, the students weren't boxed into a single learning type. They were encouraged to use whatever learning style felt most natural to them as they watched, listened, wrote, experimented, and reflected. This multisensory approach helped each child figure out what worked best for them, allowing their learning style to evolve naturally over time.

When students learn in this way, it feels natural and empowering. It builds their confidence, independence, and a deeper understanding of the material. They discover how to figure things out on their own in a way that increases their motivation.

In my videos, students could pause, practice, and then check their work as they went. They were never designed to be watched straight from start to finish. I don't know about you, but I don't think I could watch a 25-minute math video in one sitting while trying to remember every single thing I had learned along the way! I wanted the students to be able to engage with the curriculum in short chunks of two to three minutes at a time, followed by an example. They could then go to their practice problem, work it out, check their work step-by-step using the solution manual, correct their work as they went, and then return to the video when they were done. This allowed students to apply what they were learning as they went. They could interact with the curriculum while checking their understanding of the material. If you want to learn more about our video courses and how they can help your student become an independently responsible learner, visit http://www.mrdfreeresources.com.

Independently responsible learners are born when students are given the opportunity to apply what they are learning in real time. When students work through problems—checking their answers, identifying their mistakes, and returning to the lesson for clarity—they're not just practicing math; they're processing information, making connections, and reinforcing their understanding. This helps the learning stick in a way that simply reading about math never will, because reading is passive and working through a problem is active. Active learning builds confidence, retention, and comprehension. Over time, students learn to trust their own thinking because they can see the progress as it's happening!

And what happens when something isn't working? They identify the gap in their understanding and formulate a question in order to fill it. A process, prompted by their own attempts to understand the material. When students create their own questions, they are thinking independently. They're engaging with the content and not waiting for someone else to lead them to the answers or fix their mistakes. This is the heart of the independently responsible learner.

Believe it or not, it took four years for me to write five courses. Every week, I would plan lessons and create practice problems, record, edit, and then process the videos before sharing them with my students. Today, the recordings are available on an online system where students have their own unique login and password to gain access to the course materials. Over the four years it took to develop this system, I produced more than 500 videos, each designed to encourage and inspire independently responsible learners—the kind of learners and leaders we need in today's world. If you want to learn more, visit http://www.mrdfreeresources.com.

What becomes possible when a young person acts independently and responsibly? What becomes possible when students can learn freely and at their own pace? They start to do things for themselves, only asking for help if and when they need it. Instead of depending on others first, they search for their own answers, solve their own problems, think critically, and come up with their own questions when it comes time to ask for help. In other words, they realize their full potential.

When students use my method, they start taking responsibility for their own understanding of the material. They become self-directed. But this only works when students feel trusted. When students know they are trusted to try, think, and figure things out for themselves, they become more willing to take risks. They're not afraid of getting something wrong because they have learned not to see mistakes as failures. In my method, mistakes are seen as data along the way to finding the right answer; they're simply part of the process of learning.

MISTAKES

For many students, the fear of making a mistake is the very thing that stops them from trying. When they don't trust themselves or don't feel trusted by the adults teaching them, they become hesitant, passive, and sometimes even apathetic. Their natural curiosity is suppressed by a fear of failure. But when you give students room to explore, to try, and to correct themselves, they start to see mistakes differently. They begin to recognize that mistakes help them understand the work better. That discovery builds confidence—real confidence—because it comes from their own effort, rather than someone else's words.

By trusting students with the responsibility to check their own work, reflect on their mistakes, and return to the lesson when they need clarity, we're telling them, "You are capable." And when students believe they're capable, they rise to that belief. They take ownership of their work, their engagement deepens, and they learn with a new sense of freedom and confidence that stays with them long after the lesson is over.

Now consider what it really means for students to take responsibility for their learning. Think about what it would mean for your child to learn in this way. These aren't just academic skills; they're life skills. Independently responsible learners know how to analyze information, do their own research, ask meaningful questions, and think critically. They understand how to communicate more clearly, listen to explanations, see different viewpoints, discuss their ideas with others, and work collaboratively. They learn to make decisions, take initiative, and lead. These are the skills that allow young people to succeed in any environment as they come into adulthood. Who wouldn't want a person like that as an employee?

Just imagine the long-term value of these learners to our world. Picture your young person as a high school or college graduate entering the world, not just as a student, but as a uniquely capable person. They mature into an adult who knows how to conduct research, develop their own ideas, and take initiative. These types of adults can lead in any environment. Whether they choose to create their own business or start their career within an established organization, they will stand out for the better.

FROM MATH SKILLS TO LIFE SKILLS

When you look closely at the mindset of an independently responsible learner, you can begin to understand its value. I've touched on how I used these concepts to shape my math curriculum, but could these same ideas be applied to other kinds of learning and other subjects? The answer is "Yes, I've seen it happen." When I have collaborated with other teachers across disciplines in the past, we have designed curricula and programs that foster independently responsible learners in their own classrooms with great results.

In fact, the benefits of being an independently responsible learner extend far beyond school. When students become independently responsible, they gain confidence in their own abilities. And it is this confidence that allows them to go out into the world and live the life of their dreams.

Yes, it is bold of me to claim that being an independently responsible learner leads to a fuller life. Critics might say, "But where's your proof?" Well, if you want proof, try it and see for yourself. Have your young person practice being an independently responsible learner and observe the results. What evidence could be more convincing than your own experience?

But if that is not enough, let me ask you: Do you think an employer would rather hire the candidate who has memorized the most facts and formulas but lacks the flexibility to apply them in different contexts, or the one who can look for the solution to any problem, check their own work, ask for help if they need it, and correct what's not working? The independently responsible learner—the independently responsible person—can produce the results that employers want. In their personal lives, these learners are able to communicate in healthy ways, take responsibility for themselves, and become comfortable with their mistakes. This inspires others to learn from them and do the same! They can be trusted to do what is right and honorable in their word and succeed in every area of their lives. Isn't that what we all really want for our young people?

Now we must look at the role of the parent, teacher, or mentor in this transformation. When a young person begins to step into the mindset of the independently responsible learner, the adult's role must evolve with them. You're no longer going to be the one with all the answers. Instead, you must become a coach who guides their learning and asks the kinds of questions that help students discover the answers for themselves. This shift from answering questions to asking them is essential. When the adult understands how to coach instead of correct, the learner gains the space they need to take ownership of their own learning. So before we turn to the student's responsibilities as an independently responsible learner, let's take a moment to prepare you, the parent, the guide, the coach, for your own transformation.

Chapter 3

THE PARENT IS THE COACH

SHIFTING ROLES

We've focused a great deal on the learner. But what about the people supporting them? If you're a parent or a teacher, you may be wondering how best to interact with an independently responsible learner.

Up to now, you've likely thought of yourself as a teacher—someone who provides learners with instruction. But we've already seen the importance of putting learning in the hands of the student so that they can become independently responsible for their own education. Now the student must become the teacher.

So where does that leave the teacher? Where does that leave the parent? The answer lies in the concept of coaching.

A coach is more of an advisor than a task master. They help people make their own decisions, set and reach goals, and face whatever problems might arise along the way. Where a parent might lecture, a coach listens. Where a teacher might solve a problem, a coach guides their students toward solving it themselves. Where a teacher has all the answers, a coach asks all the right questions.

Your role in the life of the independently responsible learner is to be their coach. This means helping them take ownership of their own learning while standing by to guide them when they need it. The most visible aspect of this shift appears in the direction in which information flows between a coach and an independently responsible learner. In classical education models, students ask questions of teachers, but in this new model, coaches should be asking the questions and students should be answering them. Essentially, as a young person progresses toward becoming an independently responsible learner, you should feel more and more like they are teaching you, rather than the other way around.

SIGNS OF OWNERSHIP AND MASTERY

The learner's shift from student to teacher usually happens when they are asked to present their work to others. That's the moment when a coach can determine whether the learner is truly taking ownership of their work. So what should you look for as a coach? Notice the student's language and listen for phrases that indicate ownership, things like "Here's what I discovered...," "This is how I figured it out...," or "Let me show you what I learned." Pay attention to their confidence, clarity, and willingness to explain their thinking in their own words. An independently responsible learner doesn't just repeat what they have been taught; they demonstrate their understanding by teaching it back to the listener. They take the initiative to independently connect different ideas, and they formulate their own questions. These behavioral traits—confidence, curiosity, clarity, and ownership—are the signals that a learner has stepped fully into the role of the teacher and, therefore, has become an independently responsible learner.

Reflect on your interactions with your students. Are they teaching you more than you're teaching them? Have they actually mastered the course material? Can you tell that they've discovered the answers for themselves? As a coach, part of your role is to determine whether the students have actually mastered the material. If they have, it is important to specifically acknowledge their hard work. Tell them exactly what you saw: "You explained your steps clearly," or "You showed how you corrected your mistakes," or "You applied the concepts to your own example." Naming what a student did well reinforces their confidence and helps them recognize what success looks and feels like.

But what if they haven't fully mastered the information? What if something is still missing in their understanding? This is where you can step in more actively as a coach. Instead of just telling them they are wrong and giving them the answer, the coach works with the student to review their process. They ask questions like, "Where did you get stuck?" or "What part doesn't make sense yet?" or "Show me the step where things stopped working." These questions help the student pinpoint the gap in their understanding.

Then the coach must listen, really listen, to what their learners have to say. Often, the learner can explain exactly where their understanding broke down, simply because you created the space for them to slow down, consider what they'd learned, and reflect on their thought process. Through active listening, a coach allows the learner to independently step out of failure and back into discovery mode, discover what they are missing, and continue the learning process on their own initiative.

QUESTIONS INSTEAD OF ANSWERS

One of the best ways to listen as a coach is to continue asking questions. Go to **www.mrdfreeresources.com** for more information about asking questions like a coach. Below are a few coaching questions to get you started. You can use these as a guide whenever a student is struggling to understand or hasn't fully mastered the concepts they are studying.

To help them identify a gap in their understanding or a missed step:

- When did it start to feel confusing?
- Which step doesn't make sense yet?
- Show me where you got stuck.
- What changed between the part you understood and the part you didn't?

To help them revisit their thought process:

- Walk me through your steps. What were you thinking here?
- What did you expect to happen at this step?
- Does your answer make sense to you? Why or why not?

To encourage discovery instead of giving them the answer:

- What do you think your next step could be?
- What information from the lesson might be helpful here?
- If you were teaching this to someone else, what would you tell them to do next?

To build their confidence and encourage them to take ownership of their work:

- What part of this problem do you understand well?
- What have you figured out so far?
- How did you fix your last mistake?
- What can you try next?

As the coach, you'll need to practice listening and asking questions, rather than answering them. This will take practice on both your parts! You shouldn't try to correct or show them what they needed to do differently. Your job as a coach is to ask questions of the student to guide them toward understanding their mistakes. Remember, it's the student's job to discover the answers and their mistakes for themselves. Your role is to make space for their discoveries. Sometimes you might need to prompt them or ask additional questions, but now you know how to do that!

THE THREE COMMON GAPS

I have found that when students struggle to understand course material, the cause usually comes down to one of three things: clarity, connection, or completion.

Sometimes the student lacks clarity. They're not sure what a question is asking of them, or they don't understand a specific step in the process. Sometimes, they're missing a connection—they haven't linked a new idea to something they already know—so the concept feels disconnected or confusing. And sometimes they are missing completion. They may have started a problem correctly, but somewhere along the way, they skipped a step, rushed, or didn't check their work, leaving the problem unfinished. By asking questions of the student, you can help them identify which of these three pieces is missing so they can fill the gaps in their own understanding.

The independently responsible learner also learns to identify gaps in their own understanding. When they find errors in their work, they're able to discover and correct their own mistakes. Maybe they realize they skipped a step, they see that their explanation doesn't fully answer the question, or they notice that their final answer doesn't match the work they showed. When they identify what's missing—a step, a connection, or a correction—they can then go back and fix it. This process leads them to the fuller understanding they were seeking in the first place. They aren't waiting for someone else to point the way to the answer; they're learning to grow from their own mistakes.

Now, as a coach, your job is to empower, encourage, and acknowledge your student for the work they do. Support them in their own journey toward becoming an independently responsible learner. This is a lifelong practice. Why? Because we as people are always learning and growing. Independently responsible learners never stop learning, and coaches never stop coaching.

THE COACH—PLAYER ANALOGY

As the coach, you can think about this process as a sport. In this sport, our learner is your athlete on the field. They're the person participating and taking action in the match. As the coach, you're able to observe what they're doing and give them guidance from the sidelines. When a baseball player goes through a hitting slump, a coach might ask them: "What can you see in this video of yourself when you were at bat? What's missing? Where were your shoulders? Where was your elbow? Where were your eyes?"

You're not telling them where they went wrong or what they were missing. You're asking them to discover the solution for themselves. You're coaching. With time, your players learn to set goals for themselves and come up with their own solutions. If they happen to encounter a situation they can't figure out on their own, they can talk to you about it. Then you can work together to find the solution. The important thing is that through it all, the athlete is the one on the field. As the coach, you are an observer and advisor, but the athlete sets the goals and takes the actions necessary to reach them. The more you practice being a coach, the more you'll discover for yourself what it really means to be one. By discovering what a coach really is, you also demonstrate to your newly discovered, independently responsible learner that we are all, indeed, always learning.

NORMALIZING INDEPENDENTLY RESPONSIBLE LEARNERS

Step back and take on a new view of education, one in which the independently responsible learner has emerged. The more the independently responsible learner succeeds, the more others will notice and want the same thing for their own students. Before you know it, independently responsible learners will become the norm in educational spaces. This is the future of learning.

As a coach, your role in this evolution of education is critical. Thank you for taking a role in supporting and developing independently responsible learners. They are the ones who will push the limits of what is possible for generations to come.

Chapter 4

THE STUDENT IS THE TEACHER

WHY TEACHING IS THE PATHWAY TO MASTERY

You may be wondering why I keep referring to the student as a teacher. Well, if you've ever learned something on your own, done homeschooling, or taught anyone anything, you know that the best way to master a concept is by teaching it to others.

Take, for example, tying your shoes. You can show someone how to tie their shoes, or you can model it for them by tying your own shoes. However, until the person actually practices tying their shoes for themselves, they will not master the task. You are there to guide, support, and cheer them on, but it is up to the child—the learner—to figure out how to tie their own shoes. They master it through direct experience and practice. As the teacher, you are observing, coaching, and noticing what's missing for the learner. Mastery happens differently for both the learner and the person who is doing the teaching. How do you discover this idea? The way to discover this idea is to practice it. If you are a parent, have your child teach you something they learned, then have a conversation with the child about what they noticed as they were teaching the idea or concept. What did they discover for themselves by being the teacher?

When students grasp a concept, whether in math or any other subject, something powerful happens: They develop the urge to share what they have learned with others. They want to teach it back. That moment is not accidental; it's part of how real learning works. When students explain a problem in their own words, or show someone how they arrived at an answer, they're organizing their thinking and taking responsibility for their own understanding. Teaching requires clarity and confidence. The learner has to internalize a concept deeply enough to explain it to someone else. This is one of the hallmarks of an independently responsible learner.

This practice of "teaching back" the material is built directly into my courses. When students watch an example, try a problem, check their work, correct mistakes, and return to the lesson for support, they naturally reach a point where everything begins to make sense. Once that happens, teaching becomes almost instinctive. They want to say, "Let me show you what I figured out." When a student can teach a concept, they've not only mastered it, they've strengthened the very skills that make them independently responsible learners. **We've found that when students share what they're learning, it becomes part of their long-term thinking and leads to mastery.**

Many parents who homeschool their children tell me that their comprehension of a given subject was deepened through teaching it to their kids. Let's consider the neuroscience behind this phenomenon. When learners truly understand something, they can't help wanting to teach it back to you. That impulse is actually wired into the human brain. Teaching activates more areas of the brain than simply watching a video or listening to an explanation. To teach, the brain has to organize information, recall it, sequence the steps, and connect it to what it already knows. This strengthens the neural pathways that root the idea into long-term memory. This is how teaching acts as a pathway to mastery for the independently responsible learner.

MATH AS AN EXAMPLE

Let's say you are teaching someone how to add fractions together. In order to add two fractions together, one needs to find their common denominator. In the public school system, this statement is axiomatic. Teachers drill it into their students. You may even remember the term from past math classes you attended. Coaches intent on creating independently responsible learners follow a different strategy. When a coach introduces the concept of common denominators, they frame it as a question.

They ask their students to explain *why* they have to find the common denominator of two fractions before adding them together. This question is much trickier than it appears.

Imagine a coach trying to guide their student toward understanding the concept of common denominators. They start by asking the student *why* a common denominator is needed to add fractions. When the student struggles with the deceptively difficult task, a clever coach might start by presenting them with a fruit bowl.

Imagine a bowl containing three apples and five oranges. The coach might ask their student to tell them how many apples are in the bowl.

The student might count the apples and correctly answer, "Three."

"Why not eight?" the coach may ask.

"You asked about apples specifically. There were eight pieces of fruit, but only three were apples," the indignant student might argue.

At that, the sly coach might cock an eyebrow and ask: "So what does that have to do with fractions and common denominators?"

At that point, an excellent coach, well practiced in staying quiet, would sit back and let their learner begrudgingly chew on the question.

Eventually, the student might return, eyes wide with understanding. "Fruit is the common denominator." They'll excitedly declare, before elaborating further. "When you ask for the number of apples, I can't add the oranges, but when you ask for the number of fruit pieces, I can!"

The student will explain that, if one wants to add $3/8$ and $5/6$, they can think of eighths as apples and the sixths as oranges. The common denominator is fruit, or in the case of the fractions, 24ths.

By asking their student to explain *why* they needed the common denominator, rather than presenting it as an unquestioned fact, the coach led them to a much deeper understanding of not only fractions, but of mathematics in general. With the student's deeper understanding, finding the common denominator of two fractions will be more intuitive, but they are also better situated to understand more advanced concepts like unit conversions and even the quadratic formula in the future.

THE TEACH-BACK EFFECT

Teaching also gives the brain a feeling of success. When students say, "Look what I figured out!" their brains release dopamine, the neurotransmitter linked to curiosity, confidence, and motivation. This positive emotional reinforcement makes them more willing to take risks and more resilient to failure. The moment a student teaches a concept back is the moment they become independently responsible learners. They're not just repeating memorized steps; they have actually come to understand them, and the knowledge becomes natural to them.

These teachable moments are built right into my method. When students watch an example, do a practice problem, check their own work, correct their mistakes, and revisit lessons, they are setting their brains up for deeper understanding. And once that understanding clicks, teaching becomes instinctive to them. They want to communicate what they have discovered.

A PRACTICAL EXERCISE

Now it's your turn to experience this phenomenon for yourself. Here is a simple, powerful exercise you can do with your learner to see the teach-back effect in action.

Step 1: Choose a Topic

Pick any topic or let your learner choose one for themself.

Examples:

- How to reduce a fraction
- Why plants need sunlight
- How a recipe works
- What causes a rainbow
- How to solve a puzzle
- How to dribble a basketball

Step 2: Let them learn it independently.

Show them a video, give them a short reading, or let them explore the topic on their own. DON'T teach it to them. Give them the space to figure it out.

Step 3: Ask them to teach it back to you

Say: "Explain this to me as if I've never seen it before." Encourage them to use examples or to demonstrate their thinking in their own words.

Step 4: Let mistakes happen.

Seriously! Don't judge or correct them immediately. Let them process, think, check their own work, and self-correct when possible.

Step 5: Use reflective questions

Ask your student:

- "What part made the most sense to you?"
- "Did anything surprise you?"

- "What did you discover while explaining it?"
- "What would you tell someone learning this for the first time?"
- "How did it feel to teach this back?"

This tool will help you support your student as they grow into an independently responsible learner who can learn on their own, think more deeply about their opinions, and teach them back to you with confidence.

Now, will young learners—five, six, or seven years old—need some support? You bet they will. You may have to be more involved, but once they have learned the material, you can still let them try teaching it back to you. Each time they try, they gain understanding and comprehension until eventually, they master it.

Start by prompting the learner. "Here's what I would like you to discover today." "Here's what we're working on today." "Why do we need common denominators?" And leave it at that. Let them go out and find the answer. They may have to ask someone else, like a relative, sibling, classmate, or even someone working in a bank! In this day and age, they might look for help online. When they come back to you, they'll be able to explain what they have discovered. Let them deepen their own understanding by teaching it to you. However they obtained the knowledge, teaching it back to you will help them understand it better.

Do you want to teach vocabulary? Awesome. Give your learner a set of words and have them go forth and discover their definitions. Then, have them come back and teach you about the words. "Here is your vocabulary for the day. Go and find these words, find out what they mean, then come back and teach me about them."

What are they going to do? Some learners will draw pictures depicting the meanings, while others will put them in a PowerPoint to present to you.

Some might write a story about them, while others might act them out through a video recording. Other learners might go out and see where the words show up in the world, and how they're applied. They'll likely surprise you by getting far more than you expected out of a lesson on vocabulary!

BRINGING LEARNING INTO THEIR WORLD

Anyone who has spent enough time teaching has heard a student ask: "When am I ever going to use this in the real world?" As a math teacher, I get asked this question a lot.

When this question comes up, I prefer to ask, "Where is this going to show up in *your* world?" When they ask this question, what the student really wants to know is how the concepts they are learning connect to their world.

And while I could give plenty of examples, my first response for such students is usually to ask them about their interests. What is it they love to do? Once they share their response, I can ask them how they think our topic of study might show up in the things they're passionate about. This prompts them to examine themselves differently, discovering things they may not have noticed before. The honors portions of my math courses are built on this idea—having students look at what is important to them and discover how what they have been learning might apply to that world—their world. To find out more about how we teach students to integrate their education with their interests, visit **www.mrdfreeresources.com**.

Here's an example.

In our Algebra I course, we introduce the idea of "break-even points" when solving problems with variables on both sides of the equation. A break-even point can be found by using a system of equations. To solve the system, the student must find a solution that works for all of the equations at once. If you were to chart the equations as lines on a graph, the solution would be the point where they all intersect. The break-even point exercises are word problems. Here is an example of how one student, with an interest in business and economics, completed their assignment:

2.7—"Solving equations with variables on both sides."

Algebra 1

Question one: What is the title of this honors section?
The title of this honors section is: Honors credit using section 2.7 (solving equations with variables on both sides).

Question two: What did you learn about in this section?
In this section, I learned how to solve larger equations with variables on both sides instead of just one. This section taught me how to break large equations down to their components. I learned how to find the break-even point, which can be very useful in business. Overall, I learned the true importance of being able to translate words into a math equation.

Question three: What did you do well in this section?
What I did best in this section was completing the word problems on the first page of part two.

Question four: How and where can the material in this section be applied outside of a math classroom?
What I learned in this section can be applied to real-world business operations. For example, finding the break-even point of supply and demand curves can advise strategic pricing and help avoid financial losses. Knowing your break-even point helps businesses set appropriate prices. Break-even points can also

give insight into a business's viability and possibility for return on investment, making them useful to potential investors.

Isn't this what we truly want for all students—not just to learn from a book but to live it out? The student in the example not only learned about break-even points, but was also able to think of how they could be applied in the real world. Yet somewhere along the way, learning and real life became separated within our education system. We often hear the phrase "school versus the real world," as if education happens in one place and life happens in another. But the purpose of education has always been to prepare young people for the real world, not stand apart from it.

So where does this separation come from? In many traditional schooling systems, the focus has shifted over decades toward increasingly theoretical knowledge and standardized testing. Students learn how to follow steps, recite information, and pass tests, but not how to apply what they learn beyond the classroom. The connection between learning and living isn't always made clear. Maybe we, as educators, assume the applications are obvious, but for many students, they aren't. If it is never applied outside the classroom, knowledge becomes something to memorize rather than use.

When students can take what they're studying and connect it to something real, something meaningful to them, they begin to understand why it matters. They begin to see themselves in the world and see the world in what they're learning.

And this applies to every subject.

Take history, for example. If you want a young person to truly understand it, you send them to the places where history actually happened. Let them talk to people who experienced it, visit museums, walk through historic neighborhoods, or explore virtual tours of archaeological sites around the world. Technology gives us access to places and stories that were once out of reach, and if you have the means, travel can deepen the experience even further. When students have the chance to see history with their own eyes, even through a screen, they achieve deeper levels of understanding. No matter what country you may live in, you can experience the history of that country with technology today.

If a child is learning biology, give them a magnifying glass and let them explore the backyard. Have them grow a plant or watch a caterpillar become a butterfly. If they're learning geometry, let them walk through a building and identify the shapes and angles hidden in its architecture. If they're learning economics, take them grocery shopping and ask them why they think different products have different prices. If they're learning to write, let them interview a relative, write a letter, or keep a journal about their lives. The possibilities are endless.

Give a young person the chance to discover something for themselves, and you'll watch the world come alive through their eyes. They'll ask questions you didn't expect, share ideas you didn't teach them, and learn to answer their own questions. Your role as their coach becomes one of support—the person they turn to when they need guidance, instead of the source of all their information.

When you allow a student to teach you what they've discovered, you help them realize that learning is not separate from life—it is life. This is how we train young people to become independently responsible learners.

Chapter 5

CHECKING YOUR OWN WORK

WHY MOST PEOPLE WERE NEVER TRAINED TO CHECK THEIR OWN WORK

So far, we've discovered that real mastery is achieved when the student becomes the teacher. This means the student isn't just passively receiving knowledge; they're actually discovering answers—questioning and finding meaning for themselves. Checking their work and reviewing it to notice and address any mistakes or errors they made is a crucial part of this process.

This practice does not come naturally to many students, or adults for that matter. In fact, as a society, we have done a bad job at trying to understand when and how people make mistakes. This is true across all areas of life, from education to business, and even to relationships.

How many times have you suffered for a mistake you could have caught if you had just checked your work? Maybe you thought someone else would check it for you. Maybe you didn't have the skillset to do it. Maybe you weren't able to find your own mistakes because you didn't know the right answer to begin with. In my experience with my own staff, when a mistake is made, it's usually because people didn't check their work before submitting it. But why does this happen?

There are probably many reasons, but I'm going to share what I believe to be the biggest factor for why people don't check their work: They were never trained to do so. They have no experience in checking their work, so they have never developed the skills to do it themselves.

Checking your own work isn't natural; it's a skill that has to be mastered through training. And the best training moves you from learning something to knowing it.

LEARNING VS. KNOWING

Once you know something, it becomes part of who you are. We don't want people to simply learn how to check their work. Instead, we want them to *know* how to check their work. There's a difference between learning and knowing, and the best way to understand that difference is to experience it for yourself. Think about learning to swim. At first, you might memorize the steps—kick your legs, move your arms—but you don't really know how to swim until your body can move through the water without thinking about every motion. Or consider driving a car. In the beginning, you consciously learn where to place your hands, when to check your mirrors, and how to turn the wheel. But once you know how to drive, you can do it without thinking.

One way to think about it is to see "learning" as temporary and "knowing" as permanent. When you know something, you don't have to think about each step; it becomes natural and automatic. That's the level of mastery we want learners to reach, so that the skill they are trying to master becomes part of who they are.

Think about that for a moment. Checking your own work leads to mastery. Mastery leads to confidence. Confidence leads to capability, willingness, and fearlessness in the face of new challenges. The same is true when it comes to living the life of your dreams. Yes, I'm saying that checking your own work will lead you to the life of your dreams!

That might seem like a stretch, but is it really? In education today, we don't teach students how to check their own work—we do it for them, then we give it back to them and tell them to look it over in their own time.

Recall my students in the dropout prevention program from the start of my teaching career. I checked their work, made comments, and returned it to them. Do you remember what they did with it? They looked at it, looked at me, and put it away.

If you think back to your own school experience, you might remember one or two times when you actually studied the corrections your teacher made. But most of us didn't do that. The same thing often happens in homeschooling. A young person will hand in their work, get it back with markings, glance at the page, and file it away in a binder. The mistakes might be noticed, but they are not understood.

You may think, "But we go over the mistakes together!" And maybe you do. But even then, the adult ends up doing most of the thinking. The parent or teacher explains the error, how to fix it, and what the correct answer should have been. In the process, the student becomes an observer instead of a thinker. It creates more work for both people. The teacher grades the assignment and then reteaches the same lesson. The student must interpret someone else's markings rather than discovering and solving the error for themselves. The responsibility shifts away from the learner, even though the work belongs to them.

When students discover their own mistakes, the learning actually sticks!

WHAT GOES WRONG

Whose work is it anyway? If the work belongs to the student, then the responsibility for correcting it should belong to them as well. When students check their own work, they're taking responsibility, not only for getting it right but for making it right. This is where integrity comes into play.

Integrity, in this context, means wholeness and completeness. It means the student is responsible for the whole process. They turn in their work only after it has been reviewed, corrected, and understood to the best of their ability. They don't hand over a page, wondering if the answers are correct. They know what they did, they know where they made mistakes, and they know how they corrected them. The work becomes a reflection of their own thinking, not a record of someone else's red marks.

A helpful way to picture this is to imagine a bicycle wheel. When all the spokes are in place, the wheel is strong. But if some of the spokes are missing, the wheel might hold together for a while, but it will weaken over time and cannot be relied upon. It lacks integrity because essential pieces are missing.

The same is true for a student's coursework. Turning in work without checking or correcting it is like riding on a wheel with missing spokes. The page might look finished, but important pieces of understanding are absent. However, when a student checks each problem, fixes their mistakes, and makes sure they understand what they did, they're putting every spoke into place. The work becomes whole and complete, something they can trust and be proud of.

This is the kind of integrity we want students to develop in their learning. Why? Because neuroscience shows that when students identify and correct their own mistakes by checking their work, their brains create much stronger memory pathways than when the correction is given to them by a teacher. When a student notices an error, the brain sends out a "prediction error signal," like a moment of surprise that tells the brain, "Pay attention, something unexpected just happened." When the student corrects the mistake themselves, the brain strengthens the neural pathway connected to the correction in question by connecting a solution to the signal. This is another way that knowledge can move from short-term memory into long-term memory. It's the difference between something a student has learned and something they know.

MISTAKES

It is far too common in classrooms for teachers to tell students *what* they have gotten wrong, through grading and corrections, but not *how* or *why* they are wrong. Understanding that *"how"* can only come when the learner discovers their mistakes for themselves. This isn't just educational theory; it's neuroscience. When a student makes a mistake, their brain has an emotional and cognitive response. There may be a short moment of frustration, surprise, or even embarrassment. These emotions don't feel good to the student, but they serve a bigger and more powerful purpose: They alert the brain that something meaningful is happening. The emotional response heightens the student's attention, which makes the brain more receptive to learning and primes it for the creation of long-term memories.

When a student realizes their answer doesn't make sense, or that a step didn't work the way they expected, the emotional response triggers the brain to focus. When the student eventually corrects their mistake for themselves, their primed brain strengthens the neural pathway connected to whatever they were learning. Their understanding becomes clearer and more likely to stick. So yes, we learn better from our mistakes because of the emotional response associated with them. Emotions drive attention, and attention drives learning and memory.

Just as we discussed in Chapter 3, your role as a parent or educator is to be a coach. An accountability partner that offers guidance, support, and feedback as your student learns to take responsibility for their own work. You're not there to think for them. You're not there to tell them the answers. And you're not there to rescue them from every mistake. You're there to guide the education process so they can progress toward their own goals and grow into independently responsible learners.

Most of us were educated in systems where the teacher explained everything, corrected everything, and carried most of the cognitive load. Stepping back and allowing the student to take ownership doesn't always feel natural at first. Adults generally need practice to get better at letting their students struggle a little, reflect, discover, and correct on their own.

So how do you "get it right" as the coach? Remember the questions we discussed in Chapter 3. You don't need the right answers, you need the right questions—questions that encourage thinking. The more you practice this approach, the easier it will become for you and your students.

If you're an educator, mentor, or parent who wants to develop these coaching skills, skills that help students grow into confident, self-directed learners, I'd love to hear from you. Reach out to explore how you can begin integrating these methods into your own teaching practice and empower your students to take responsibility for their own learning. Visit **www.mrdfreeresources.com** to learn more.

In the next chapter, we'll explore why learning to present their work is one of the most powerful steps a student can take in becoming an independently responsible learner.

Chapter 6

PRESENT YOURSELF

SPECIAL INSTRUCTIONS: The bulk of this book is written for adults who want to foster independently responsible learning in their students. This chapter, however, is intended for the learners themselves. If you're an adult reading this, approach it as the student would, or better yet, allow yourself to be the student. Who knows, maybe the learner in your life will want to read this chapter too!

WHAT THIS REALLY MEANS

The word "present" has many definitions. It could refer to a state of mindfulness or the act of presenting something to an audience. Let's consider both of these definitions because they all apply to the mindset of the independently responsible learner.

So, what does it mean to present yourself?

Presenting yourself is about more than just handing in an assignment. It means showing up fully, being aware, engaged, and ready to communicate what you've learned. It means taking ownership of the work you've done and explaining your thought process, rather than simply showing your answers. Presenting yourself also means advocating for the effort you put in. It's the ability to say, "Here is what I've done, here is what I discovered, and here is why it matters."

By presenting what you have learned, you make it your own. When you present, you translate your discoveries into your own words—you take ownership of your education through sharing it with others. This is how learners develop pride and integrity in their work. When you present your work, you're demonstrating that you understand it, you've taken responsibility for it, and you're willing to stand behind it.

But how does this relate to the mindfulness definition of "present"?

Think back to a time when you led something—a discussion group, a workshop, a class activity, or even a Zoom meeting. Sharing your thoughts with others shifted something inside you. You were the one speaking. You were the one leading. You were responsible. And because of that, you became more present. Your attention was fully focused on what you were doing and saying. When you're present while presenting, your mind isn't drifting or distracted. You're right there, fully engaged in the moment. Your entire focus is narrowed in on what you're communicating. This experience is closely connected to what psychologists call a flow state.

FLOW STATE

The term "flow state" refers to the mental state you enter when you become so focused on what you're doing that you forget about everything else. Time, noise, distractions, and even self-doubt all fade into the background as your focus stays on the task at hand. Athletes feel it during a match, musicians feel it while performing, and you might feel it while working on a project you love. The flow state happens when your actions align with your purpose.

As a learner, presenting your own work can create the same flow-like experience. When you're explaining something you understand, you aren't thinking about how you're saying it; you're just saying it. You're not repeating someone else's words; you're explaining your own understanding of the material. You're choosing your own language, organizing your own thoughts, and taking responsibility for what you're communicating. That is the power of being present and being in flow. It transforms the learner from someone who passively completes assignments into someone who can actively communicate their discoveries.

Finding the flow state as a presenter is not always easy. You must hone your ability to express your own ideas with clarity and confidence. That skill doesn't appear all at once; it grows each time you take what you've learned and translate it into something you can confidently communicate to someone else—something you can teach back. The more you practice presenting, the more natural and "in flow" it will begin to feel.

Now let's go a level deeper to better understand the different forms a presentation can take.

MULTIPLE INTELLIGENCES

Every student has unique skills and unique ways of expressing themselves. When you present your work, it's important to recognize that you do not need to fit yourself into someone else's mold. Your presentation should be a reflection of yourself, not your audience. Not every idea should be presented the same way, either. Some topics are best explained verbally, some visually, some through demonstration, and others through storytelling or examples.

What we're really looking to do is develop your communication skills as a learner—your ability to take what you've discovered and express it in a form that makes sense to you. That's why no two students' presentations should look the same. The act of presenting makes the knowledge your own. Identifying, developing, and owning your personal communication style is part of growing into an independently responsible learner.

Educational researcher Howard Gardner beautifully describes this in his theory of multiple intelligences. He explains that people learn and express themselves through different natural strengths. Some students are great with words, others understand the world through numbers and logic. Some think visually, while others learn best through movement, music, or tangible experiences. Some learners process ideas quietly and internally, and still others think best by talking things out with a peer. When you understand your strengths, your presentations can become an extension of how you naturally learn and express yourself.

- If you're a verbal or linguistic learner, your strength might be in explaining your thinking through clear communication and storytelling.
- If you're more logic-driven or mathematically-minded, you might show your understanding through patterns, examples, and step-by-step reasoning.
- If you're a visual-spatial learner, you might create diagrams, drawings, or models to present your ideas.
- If you're a bodily-kinesthetic learner, demonstrating a process physically or using hands-on examples might make the most sense to you.
- If you're musically inclined, rhythm or song may help you explain your ideas.
- If you're social (interpersonal), discussions or teaching others may be your strength.
- If you're more reflective (intrapersonal), you might choose a thoughtful written or recorded explanation that explains your internal process.

When you present your work in a way that complements your strengths, your ideas come alive and become uniquely your own. The presentation stops being an assignment and becomes a form of self-expression. Your work should sound like you, look like you, and demonstrate how you think.

CREATIVE FORMATS: SLIDES, VIDEOS, MODELS, SONGS, PROJECTS, AND MORE

Depending on your learning style, you may want to use different presentation formats. As a visual learner, with a visual learner for a daughter, I have always been partial to digital slideshow presentations.

In order to create a slideshow, a student must first become proficient with whichever software they are using to build it. They might learn to use transitions or timers between slides, figure out how to include graphics and images, or even embed video clips and animations. Whatever they decide to do, they're adding elements of their own interests to bring their presentations to life!

If you've never experimented with PowerPoint before, it's the software I use to create most of my slideshows and a great way to practice presenting your work. You can build individual slides for each step of a problem, using colors, arrows, or animations to show how each idea links to the next one. From the time my daughter was 8, she created and presented a weekly PowerPoint slideshow about everything she had learned that week. Now, as a college student, she already has a decade of experience in creating and presenting her ideas. The head start she got from this weekly ritual almost makes up for all the clashing color schemes and unrelated photos of puppies I had to endure during those early years. In all seriousness, don't hesitate to add your own flair to your presentation. Remember that they should be just as much a reflection of yourself as they are of the material you have learned.

But when it comes to presentation formats, the possibilities are endless. Tactile learners can build LEGO models to demonstrate various concepts, like fractions or ratios. Or they could record themselves baking cookies while explaining the math behind the measurements, conversions, and scaling-up of recipes. I once had a student who made a stop-motion video to demonstrate how algebraic expressions change when you substitute numbers. You could create comic strips, flowcharts, posters, diagrams, and even songs to teach a concept. Maybe you're a very kinesthetic learner, someone who needs to be hands-on and outside. If so, you could take someone outside on a walk so they can physically explore and touch whatever it is you're presenting about. The point is, by presenting your work in your own unique way, you're developing your self-expression and experiencing the true joy of learning. You're developing communication skills and learning how to make sense of your ideas and share them with someone else. However you choose to communicate and present your work, it's an opportunity to practice being an independently responsible learner.

PRESENTATIONS AS PREPARATION

Presenting your work doesn't just prepare you for exams and assessments—it prepares you for life. More specifically, it prepares you for life beyond the classroom and beyond schooling. The same skills that make for good presenters in school also make for high performers in the workplace. They open you up to a world of careers where you can create, collaborate, communicate, and take initiative. These are the kinds of habits and skills that allow students to discover their personal learning styles, their inspirations, and maybe even their aspirations. The better you understand your own strengths and passions, the more likely you will be to find a career where you can thrive.

There are discoveries to be made about what it means to be an independently responsible learner that extend far beyond the classroom. And the best way to understand this next step is not to read about it, but to experience it for yourself.

A PERSONAL ASSIGNMENT

I am going to give you an assignment to help you practice presenting yourself like an independently responsible learner. Choose something you've learned recently, anything at all. It could be something you learned in school, but remember that learning is a lifelong pursuit. You could choose a recipe you mastered, a new piece of technology you figured out, a book you read, a skill you practiced, or even something you discovered while reading this very chapter. Now create a short presentation about what you learned. It doesn't need to be fancy. It can be a slideshow, a written explanation, a short video, a demonstration, or simply a face-to-face conversation.

Now present it to someone. Be present while presenting it, and notice what happens inside you.

After the presentation, take a moment to reflect:

- What did presenting help you understand more clearly about the subject?
- What parts flowed naturally when you explained them?
- How did teaching it help you see the material differently?
- What did you know after presenting that you hadn't learned before?

If you are a teacher or parent, by experiencing this process for yourself, you'll be able to explain it far more powerfully to the learners in your life. You'll understand—not just in theory, but in practice—how presenting turns learning into knowing, and why this step is an essential part of being an independently responsible learner. If you are a learner, you just discovered all of this for yourself!

These are life skills—they stay with students long after the lesson ends.

When you learn to present your work—to defend it, communicate it clearly, and take responsibility for your understanding—you gain a level of confidence and mastery that goes far beyond the content of the presentation itself. You learn to trust your thinking and how to show what you know. Those skills are especially important in the one place where many students feel the most pressure in their education: tests.

Testing is another kind of presentation. It may not involve slides, videos, or creative demonstrations, but it does require you to present your knowledge. Like any academic presentation, tests are a way for the student to show their understanding, just in a very rigid format.

And just like presenting your work, testing becomes easier and less stressful when you take responsibility for your learning. In the next chapter, we're going to be talking about how to prepare for and take tests as an independently responsible learner.

Chapter 7

TESTING, TESTING, 1–2–3

TESTS IN SCHOOL AND IN LIFE

So now that you've explored how to be present and how to present yourself, it's time to take those same strengths into one of the most common and often feared parts of education: the test.

Testing, testing, 1-2-3. You've heard that phrase before.

I'll get to the 1-2-3 soon, but for now, let's take a look at what I mean by testing.

People say that life is a test. A test of what? A test of many things. Just think about the many kinds of tests that you will take throughout your lifetime, both in and out of school.

When people think of testing, they often think about aptitude tests, like the SAT or the ACT. These are designed to predict how well the student taking the test will do in college. Then there are achievement tests, like the end-of-year tests taken by both homeschoolers and public schoolers alike. Typically, these tests compare you to others in your age group or grade level and rank you accordingly. Finally, there are the tests you take in school, like unit tests, final exams, and the dreaded pop quizzes that you can't prepare for.

Now, you likely associate all of those tests with school. For adults, they probably all bring back memories—both good and bad! If you're a student, they might make you think of the future because you know that those tests, and many more, are on the way.

These are all academic tests, the kind of tests we immediately think of when we hear the word. But tests don't just end in school. Life is full of them!

Anyone in the US with a driver's license has taken a driving test with both a written and a road component. If you're going to join the military, there is a test you must take before being able to join. There is also a test for First Aid and CPR certification. Even SCUBA divers need to take a test to be certified for open water diving!

What about professional career tests? Many careers require adults to take tests before they can even begin working in their field. Lawyers take the Bar Exam, doctors must pass medical licensing exams, and nurses take the National Council Licensure Exam, which is the official exam that all nursing graduates in the United States and Canada must pass before they can practice. People who become accountants take the CPA exam, teachers must take certification exams for their subject areas, and real estate agents must pass a licensing test before they can sell a single home. People earn certifications in areas like cloud computing, cybersecurity, software development, and project management. Other professions require safety or compliance exams. Commercial truck drivers take the Commercial Driver's License test, firefighters and EMTs must pass rigorous certification exams, and restaurant workers often have to complete food-safety training assessments.

Even during the hiring process, many employers use tests to evaluate applicants: typing tests, customer-service scenarios, logic assessments, coding challenges, or writing samples can all appear in interviews. And in certain high-pressure professions—law enforcement, military, and even astronauts—psychological and personality testing is often a requirement of employment. Even after people begin working, many careers require ongoing testing to keep licenses current or demonstrate continued competence. There is testing, testing, and more testing. Testing, testing, 1-2-3!

Simply put, testing is just as much a part of adult life as it is of childhood. And when students learn to check their work, present it, and become independently responsible learners, they grow into competent professionals who test easily and without stress.

Given that tests are such a ubiquitous part of life, it is important to have the tools to approach them with confidence. In the next sections, I will share three secrets that will help you prepare for any test.

SECRET #1: MAKE IT IMPORTANT

Testing, testing, 1-2-3. There are three secrets to all types of test-taking, no matter who is taking it or what type of test it is.

Secret number one: The test is important.

Now, what do I mean by that? I mean, make it important! I like to use the SAT as an example. When facing the SAT, I ask students a series of questions that go something like this: "Why are you taking the SAT?" The answer is usually related to getting into college or earning a scholarship. I always push harder. "Why are you going to college?" The answer generally relates to the student wanting a great job in the future. "Why do you want a great job?" The answer almost always relates to income. "Why do you want to have a great income?" Most students reply that they want a great income to allow them to take care of their family, travel, and have nice things.

Ultimately, my students are telling me that they are taking the SAT in order to live an amazing life. That tells me that, to the students, the SAT leads to living an amazing life. When these stakes are made explicit, students often find it much easier to prioritize the SAT in their lives.

The driving test is also important. If you pass the test, you get your driver's license and all the freedom and opportunities that go along with it. If you don't pass the test, you miss out on all of that. If you want to join the military, your scores on the entrance exams will determine your placement and, possibly, the trajectory of your entire career.

All tests, regardless of the specifics, determine what comes next for you in one way or another. If you can start to understand this, you will naturally prioritize them. If you say it's important to you, you'll prepare for it like it's important to you, and you'll be better prepared to take it when the time comes.

Part of making the test important in your life is practicing for it. If the test is important to you, give it the time and energy it deserves. Take practice tests to identify your weak areas and study to strengthen them. Remember that however much you prepare for a test is an expression of how important it is to you.

If you'd like assistance with putting these ideas into practice, or you want your learner to experience this method firsthand, visit www.mrdfreeresources.com for more information on how I can help.

Secret number two is the biggest secret of all. I don't only teach this one to my students, but their parents and my staff as well!

SECRET #2: FIND THE QUESTION FIRST, THEN ANSWER THE PROBLEM

Secret number two: You have to identify the question before you can begin to answer it. You may be thinking to yourself, "How is that a secret?" It seems obvious. Well, let's look at how you've been trained to approach exam problems.

When faced with a test problem, we've always been taught to start by reading everything from the beginning to the end—but that just doesn't work for most kids. Exam problems, especially word problems, generally consist of a description of a situation followed by a question at the end. Notice that I am using the word "problem" and not "question." This is because the problem is the entirety of whatever...well, "problem"...you're working on. The question is an important part of the problem.

When I tell students to identify the question first, I mean that they should determine what the problem is asking, before wading into the details. Once students know the question, they can go back and figure out how to answer it using the rest of the information provided in the problem.

Students tell me all the time that this secret makes a huge difference for them on tests. There are merits for reading everything from start to finish, but focusing the mind on the question helps students pick out the important details from a word problem.

I've looked at hundreds of math books and seen so many different techniques for solving word problems. My personal favorite was a particularly complicated eight-step process, which gave me a good laugh. Eight steps to do a word problem!? At that point, it would probably be more efficient to just wing it! By the time you figure out the eight-step plan, you likely could have already completed the word problem!

All joking aside, every textbook's approach to word problems had the same first step: Start at the beginning and read all the way to the end. I know from experience that this doesn't work. Students struggle to distinguish relevant from irrelevant information. Often, the question itself is lost in the clutter of the word problem as a whole. This is why I have students reverse the process by looking at the question first. If students start at the end, they know what to look for when they go back to the start of the problem to gather whatever information is needed to find the solution.

Who taught you to begin a test by reading everything from beginning to end before starting a test? It was likely a teacher, parent, or other authority figure.

Now, consider who taught your teacher to do it that way? It was most likely their own school teachers. This has been going on for generations. We have been perpetuating the same ineffective methods of learning and hobbling students with outdated techniques. Let me explain.

When we read something, we don't actually read every single word. Our brains interpret sentences by recognizing known patterns of words and interpreting meaning from those patterns. Let me give you an example.

Read what you see in the box below out loud to yourself.

Paris in the the spring XO XO

If you said it reads, "Paris in the spring xo xo," how surprised would you be to know that that is *not* actually what it says? Look again. Can you spot what it really says? This time you'll notice that it actually reads "Paris in the the spring xo xo." Did you miss the second "the" the first time you read it?

When we read, we make assumptions about the text based on our past experience. We drop the second "the," so to speak. In testing, you might make assumptions about the problem you're solving before you've even seen the question. You're forming opinions. So what is wrong with forming an opinion about the problem you're working on? When you're taking a test, your opinion doesn't matter. The objective of the test is to answer as many questions correctly as possible.

In tests, the question is almost always found at the end of the problem, after all the background information. If you read the problem from start to finish, you likely won't be able to distinguish the important information from the background by the time you reach the question. You might think you have an idea of what the problem is talking about, but when you go to answer the question, you'll end up misunderstanding it.

Just think about how often you've taken a test or assessment, maybe even been in a conversation with someone, and you've answered a different question from the one that was asked of you. If you form an opinion about the problem before reading the question, by the time you reach the end, you'll already have come up with your own question. You'll miss the question the problem is actually asking, and answer the one you assumed they were asking instead.

So, how do you find the question? Follow the punctuation! English grammar is an amazing thing. We make it easy for readers to identify questions at a glance by looking for question marks. If there is a question mark in the problem, that is where the question will be. If there isn't a question mark in the problem, then you might need to look for a command or instruction.

Take a look at these examples.

"If a triangle has sides measuring 10 inches, 12 inches, and 14 inches, what is the perimeter of the triangle?"

The question is right there at the end: *What is its perimeter?* The question mark tells you exactly what you're being asked to find.

Sometimes, there is extra information in the problem that you don't need at all.

"A square and a triangle are placed side by side. The square measures 10 inches on each side. The triangle also measures 10 inches on each side. What is the perimeter of the triangle?"

Notice that the information about the square is not needed to answer the question of finding the perimeter of the triangle.

Sometimes test questions don't include a question mark. In that case, the problem may end with a command or instruction instead. For example:

"Simplify the expression below." or "Solve for x." or "Write your answer in simplest form."

These don't use question marks, but they still tell you exactly what you're expected to do. They are action statements—directions that take the place of a question.

Most of the time, whether it's a question mark or a command, the thing you're supposed to solve is written not at the beginning but the end of the problem. The beginning often gives the information, details, or story of the problem. The end tells you the assignment.

For example: "*A store is having a 25% off sale on all items. If a jacket originally costs $48, find the sale price.*"

See what happens? The story comes first, and the question comes last: *Find the sale price.*

Once you train yourself to look for the question or the instruction—especially at the end—you immediately know what the problem is asking. And once you know what the problem is asking, everything else becomes much easier.

So find the question. Once you find the question, you can go back into the problem and look for the information you need to answer the question you found. But with the question in mind, you can read with more intention and distinguish the important information from any distractions. The word intention means to direct the mind to something.

When you read the problem with intention, you orient your mind toward answering the question. You're looking for the information that will assist you in your intention and ignoring information that will not. This takes practice. Why? Because we've been training people not to take tests this way for hundreds of years.

This pattern of teaching didn't appear out of nowhere—it originally taught students an important skill that has become increasingly less important over time. The method originated in a time when memorization wasn't just a helpful tool; it was a necessity. Think about what education looked like 200 years ago. There was no internet. No smartphones. No Google. No quick way to look something up. Paper was expensive, and writing was done almost entirely at large desks. People couldn't carry complete encyclopedias on ships crossing the ocean or take a library with them as they traveled. If you didn't memorize information, you simply didn't have access to it. As a result, education was centered on recalling facts, reciting passages, copying notes, and reading everything in order, because that was the only way to preserve and pass along knowledge.

Back then, reading from the beginning made perfect sense. That is the best way to memorize a passage. But today, that mentality actually gets in the way of effective test-taking. Take a reading comprehension passage. Most students begin by reading every word from the beginning, hoping they'll be able to keep all of the information straight by the time they reach the end. That's the old memorization model. But strong test-takers do something completely different: They look at the question first. If the question asks, *"What is the author's main argument?"* they know exactly what to look for. They read with intention and focus their attention on the portions of the passage that help them answer the question!

Consider a math word problem: *A train leaves the station at 7:45 traveling 60 miles per hour...*

Most students dive into the story from the top. But confident test-takers scan to the end first, looking for question marks:

"How far does the train travel in 2.5 hours?"

Now they know which information matters and which can be ignored, and they can go about looking for ways to solve the problem.

The outdated test-taking model was made for a world that relied on memorization, but today we live in a time when information is readily available—A time when skills like analysis, synthesis, and problem-solving are more important than pure memorization.

As with so many aspects of the independently responsible learner model, Secret #2 is easily applied outside the classroom as well. Let's look at a few examples.

Imagine you're auditioning for a play. Wouldn't you want to know what the director is looking for in an actor before you audition? What is the question? The question becomes: What kind of person is this director looking to cast? Regardless of the problem, the first step must be to find the question.

What if you're given a map and asked to create directions for a trip? Don't you need to know where you're going first? We need to know the question—the destination—before we can come up with the directions.

So what have we done so far? We've discovered that secret #1 is: The test is important. We've discovered that secret #2 is: You must find the question first, then read the problem to help you answer it.

Now for the third secret.

SECRET #3: TEACH AT LEAST TWO PEOPLE WHAT YOU'RE PRACTICING

The third secret is: When practicing for a test, teach two other people what you're studying. Just like we covered in Chapter 4, the student must become the teacher in order to master the material.

This third secret brings the other two together. You're practicing and refining your understanding of the material by teaching someone else what you've discovered. Additionally, sharing your knowledge with others makes accuracy even more important. Remember, the independently responsible learner actualizes their learning by sharing it.

So now you know the three secrets to test-taking.

SECRET #1: The test is important.

SECRET #2: Find the question and then answer the question.

SECRET #3: Teach at least two other people what you've learned.

In the next chapter, we're going to explore thinking. Learning is all about thinking.

Chapter 8

LEARNING HOW TO THINK

TRADITIONAL LEARNING TRAINS MEMORIZING, NOT THINKING

Modern education systems do not give students many opportunities to actually learn how to think. Now, that's an odd statement, I know. What do I mean? Well, if you look at the education system, there's not much emphasis on critical thinking.

What if we stopped to think about thinking for a moment? A great question to start with is: "How do you learn to be a great thinker?"

Today, education is very mechanical. We have numerous distinct "subjects." Within each, we practice problems, we memorize facts, and then we take assessments to prove our comprehension. There is not much room to practice thinking in that equation.

When we talk about thinking, we have to acknowledge that everyone thinks differently. The first step to helping someone learn to think is to identify their learning style.

There are many assessments out there that can help you determine your learning style, so I'm not going to recommend any one in particular. You could go online to find a free assessment, or find a professional and pay them to figure out your learning style for you. I have also included an informal exercise later in this chapter that can help you get started. But what happens after you identify your learning style? How do you use your learning style to your advantage as a thinker and independently responsible learner?

As I mentioned in Chapter 6, much of modern education still relies on passive learning—listening, memorizing, reciting, and following rigid steps without asking why. Students are taught to consume information, not to question it. They read from the beginning, move through the material in order, and hope they understand it by the time they reach the end. That isn't thinking; it's following.

Thinking is different—it is active. Thinking requires noticing, questioning, discovering, and connecting all that you learn. When you're thinking, you're no longer just taking in information—you're using it. That's the heart of the independently responsible learner.

DISCOVERING YOUR LEARNING STYLE

Now, this brings us back to the idea of learning styles. Many people believe that once they know their learning style, the work is done. But simply knowing your learning style doesn't make you a thinker. And it certainly should not define or limit your potential—it's meant to give you insight into how your brain naturally learns best.

My courses do not assume that students already know their own learning style. In fact, most students don't actually know how they learn best, and that's completely fine. The work we're going to do next will help you discover it for yourself.

Before we move forward, I'm going to give you a simple exercise to help you determine your learning style. This will allow you to see not only how you learn, but also how you think, how you discover, and how you make meaning out of new information.

Once you understand it, you'll be able to use your learning style as a tool to become a stronger, more independently responsible learner. Are you ready?

Describe your perfect day.

Take a moment to imagine it. Think about where you are, what you're doing, and how the day unfolds.

Now I'm going to ask you a series of supplementary questions. Each group of questions aligns with a different learning style. Pay attention to which questions resonate with you because that will provide insight into how you naturally think and learn.

LEARNING QUESTIONS

---

1. Visual Learning Style Questions

Visual learners understand best by seeing images, pictures, details, and structures.

If these questions help you describe your perfect day, you likely lean toward visual learning:

- What do you see on your perfect day?
- What does your perfect day look like from the moment you wake up?
- What colors, places, or scenes stand out?
- If your perfect day were a picture, what would be in it?

These questions work because visual learners organize information through images and patterns in what they *see*. If visual questions bring your perfect day into focus, it suggests that you process information visually.

2. Auditory Learning Style Questions

Auditory learners connect ideas through sound, conversation, and language.

If these questions make your perfect day come alive, you may be an auditory learner:

- What does your perfect day sound like?
- Who are you talking to?
- What conversations or words are part of your day?
- Is there music, quiet, laughter, or background noise?

These questions work because auditory learners understand best when ideas are spoken, heard, or verbalized. If sound-based questions help you deepen your description, this style is likely a good fit for you.

3. Kinesthetic Learning Style Questions

Kinesthetic learners think through movement, action, and physical experiences.

If these questions help you describe your perfect day, you may be a kinesthetic learner:

- What are you doing during your perfect day?
- How does your body move throughout the day?
- What activities or actions are part of your experience?
- What are you touching, exploring, or physically interacting with?

These questions work because kinesthetic learners discover meaning through doing. Through physical sensation, activity, and tangible hands-on experience.

4. Emotional / Internal (Intrapersonal) Learning Style Questions

Some learners process the world through feelings, values, and inner reflection.

If these questions help you imagine your perfect day more deeply, you may lean toward intrapersonal learning:

- How would you feel on your perfect day?
- What emotions are part of that experience?
- What values are present in your perfect day?
- What makes that day meaningful to you?

These questions work because internal learners discover meaning from the inside out. Emotion-centered questions give them clarity and direction.

As you read through the above questions, notice which ones helped you experience your perfect day more clearly.

- Did the image-based questions work best?
- Did sound and words make it clearer?
- Did physical action bring it into focus?
- Did emotions give you the strongest insight?

Whichever group of questions brought your perfect day to life is likely connected to your learning style. And when you understand how you learn, you can think more clearly and ask better questions. Once a student knows their learning style, they can also use these kinds of guiding questions whenever they're stuck, confused, or trying to understand something new.

USING YOUR LEARNING STYLE

Now that you have a better understanding of your learning style, you need to know how to use it. Your learning style isn't meant to label you; it's meant to guide you. When you know how you naturally take in information, you can employ learning strategies that support the way your brain learns best. If you're a visual learner, you can use diagrams, charts, color-coding, or visual examples to understand a concept. If you're an auditory learner, you can read out loud, talk through problems, or listen to explanations. If you're a kinesthetic learner, you can use hands-on tools, build models, move while you study, or physically interact with problems. If you're an internal/emotional learner, you can connect ideas to values, feelings, or personal meaning to deepen your understanding.

Whatever your style, the point is that your learning style is not the end of your learning; it's the beginning of thinking.

Test-taking becomes far easier when you use your learning style to your advantage. The moment you find the question in a problem, you can bring your learning style into the process of answering it.

Here's what that looks like in a test-taking scenario:

Visual Learners

- Underline key words in the question.
- Picture the problem as a diagram or scene.
- Imagine what the solution "looks like" before writing it down.

Auditory Learners

- Whisper the question to yourself (silently is fine!)
- "Hear" yourself talk through the steps.
- Turn the problem into a sentence or explanation in your mind.

Kinesthetic Learners

- Trace the steps with your finger.
- Use scratch paper to physically move through the problem.
- Treat each step like an action—something you do, not just think.

Internal/Emotional Learners

- Connect the question to something meaningful. For example, ask yourself, "What is this problem really about?"
- Check how the solution "feels." Does it feel complete, or does something seem off?

Using your learning style during a test will help you stay calm and focused—which is essential for effective test-taking. Rather than just reading and reacting, you can think clearly and direct your mind with purpose.

HOW LEARNING STYLES SUPPORT INDEPENDENTLY RESPONSIBLE LEARNING

The independently responsible learner doesn't wait for someone else to explain what they need to do. They use their learning style to guide themselves. They know how to ask the kinds of questions that unlock their own understanding. They know how they think and learn best.

And because of that, they can:

- Check their own work
- Correct their mistakes
- Present their thinking clearly
- Take tests with confidence
- Trust their own understanding
- Stay present—not panicked—during challenges
- Turn learning into knowing

Learning styles help students take ownership of their learning because they give them a way to navigate information independently in a form that feels natural. Instead of feeling stuck, overwhelmed, or passive, students who know their learning style can take the lead in their own education. Independently responsible learners use their learning styles as a tool to help them think and understand without relying on someone else to do it for them. The ability to guide yourself through learning, discovering, correcting, understanding, and presenting, all without relying on someone else to do the thinking for you, is central to what an independently responsible learner is.

KNOWING HOW YOU THINK

Knowing how to think is the first step toward understanding yourself. Once you know your learning style, you'll start noticing what sparks your curiosity. Thinking isn't something that "just happens." It's a skill you must develop through practice.

Some people think most clearly when they sit quietly by themselves, letting their thoughts unfold. Others discover their ideas through writing, journaling, reflecting, or organizing their thoughts on paper. Still, others think best while moving, walking, exercising, or spending time outside.

Thinking is fueled by curiosity. It requires the learner to get curious about the questions that come up for them when they learn something new. But to be a great thinker, you must also learn to listen to yourself and others. When you listen to your own thoughts, you learn to notice your own personal patterns, reactions, and how your ideas naturally form. When you listen to others, you begin to understand varying perspectives, emotions, and deeper meanings that may not have been obvious to you at first.

There are different ways to listen to yourself. You can start by asking:

- How does this make me feel? (emotional or internal learners)

- What does this look like to me? (visual learners)

- How does this sound when I say it, or when I hear it? (auditory learners)

- How can I interact with this idea or do something with it? (kinesthetic learners)

The question you respond to most naturally is generally the one that aligns with your learning style. Learning how to think means learning how to guide your mind.

One thing I can tell you is that the best person on the planet to learn about you is you. There's no one else like you. You're unique, wonderful, amazing, brilliant, and talented. The one universal constant that I've noticed from years of being in education around different cultures and people is that we all just want to make a difference in the world. We all just go about it in our own unique ways.

Chapter 9

DO WHAT YOU LOVE TO DO

INTERVIEWS WITH SUCCESSFUL PEOPLE

Several years ago, I interviewed a group of very successful people. I wanted to discover what about them allowed them to achieve the kind of success they had created in their lives. Among them was an engineer, a real estate professional, and the owner of a car dealership.

I thought, surely there must be some secret that allowed all three of them to be so successful. Was it because they had gone to college? Or was it linked to where they had grown up? Maybe it was the culture they grew up in? Perhaps it was related to the friends they kept, the people they associated with, or what they had studied. Or maybe they just worked their way up through pure grit. I thought their "Aha!" moments may have come during school or when they first started in their careers.

It turns out that when I asked them, I discovered my trio of successes had little in common. Two went to college, and one did not. One grew up in the United States, and two grew up in other countries. Two came from very happy and loving families, and one didn't. One had lots of brothers and sisters, the others did not. So what was it that they all had in common? They all loved what they did.

The real estate agent told me that his biggest thrill in life was putting together a real estate deal. He loved bringing buyers and sellers together. The engineer loved creating new ways to do things that haven't been thought of before. He embraced his creativity and then figured out how to make his idea real for others.

The car dealer wanted his customers to have the perfect car, but it wasn't just about that for him. His favorite part of the job was going to auctions and finding amazing vehicles that no one else saw the value in.

He loved finding great deals on cars that he could buy, fix up, and resell to someone else.

This pattern of loving their jobs held true for all the successful people I interviewed.

PERSONAL STORY

When I was growing up, I knew I was going to go to college, but I wasn't certain whether I would be able to study something I loved. In my generation, people didn't ask, "What do you love to do?" In fact, most of the time we were told that what we loved to do should be a hobby, not a job. For example, if you loved music (like I did), you were told that music could be a great hobby, but you still had to find a "real job."

So, I went to college. I didn't focus on what I wanted to do but rather what I thought I was *supposed* to do. What did I want to be when I "grew up?" I knew I loved to teach, and I knew that I loved music. But I had already convinced myself that I couldn't become a music teacher or a music major. I also knew that teachers weren't paid a decent wage. So my first degree in college was not in education—it was in business administration. But right after college, I went to work for a major corporation and quickly discovered I wasn't happy with my career path. It wasn't until a few years later that I went back to college to get my teaching credentials, and later earned a Master's Degree in Education.

I now know that what I really love to do is perform. I've always loved it. And when teaching, I get the chance to perform all the time. When I play music, I get the chance to perform. By writing this book, I get the chance to perform. I am a performer. If you had told me when I was younger, "You're going to be a performer," then maybe I would have gone into the movie business and become an actor. But as I said, at that time, children weren't encouraged to do what they loved. It wasn't considered sensible.

But the signs were there. When I was a little boy, only three or four years old, I would carry a little brown suitcase all through the house, taking it wherever I went. I would go into a room, put the suitcase down, stand on top of it, and announce: "Introducing Mr. Denny! Introducing Mrs. Mommy! Introducing Mr. Daddy! Introducing Mr. B!" (My brother's name is Steve, and I couldn't say Steve, so I said B.)

I was performing! And I enjoyed doing it. I look at my life today, and one of my favorite things to do as a teacher is to perform. I love to be in front of people. Whether I'm teaching, playing an instrument, singing, or speaking to groups of people at a convention, I love to perform! In fact, I think it's what I was born to do.

When I say I'm a performer as a teacher, I don't just mean being animated or enthusiastic, although that's certainly part of it. What I mean is that teaching, for me, is an experience of being fully alive in front of the people I'm working with. It's about bringing energy and presence to every lesson, using my voice, my expressions, my movement, and even my humor to draw students in so they feel like they're part of something unfolding right in front of them. Think about a great performer on stage, the way they hold your attention, the way they make you feel included in the moment. That's what teaching feels like to me.

I love guiding students through a discovery, rather than simply explaining new information. Sometimes that means telling a story that lights up an idea, pacing across the room as we build a concept together, or pausing as an actor would, to let something important sink in. My classrooms are often filled with laughter, questions, surprises, and those electric moments when a student's eyes light up as a concept finally shifts into focus. Those moments are my standing ovations.

In a movie like *Dead Poets Society*, you see a teacher who uses passion and participation to awaken something inside his students. I'm not saying I taught on desks, although I have been known to move around when teaching and have never enjoyed standing still at a podium. I strive to bring that same kind of energy: The belief that learning is not a quiet, mechanical process, but something that can be vibrant, joyful, expressive, and deeply human.

For me, performing as a teacher means showing up fully and inviting my students to do the same.

So, what is it that you love to do?

"IF YOU DO WHAT YOU LOVE, THE MONEY WILL FIND YOU"

Remember the three successful people I interviewed? I mentioned what the car salesman and real estate agent said they loved about their jobs, but I left out the engineer. Now, let's talk about him. When I asked the engineer what he loved to do, he told me he loved to design and create computer programs. He was also really great at it. He worked on the initial software of one of the first-ever voice over IP (VoIP) phone systems. During our interview, he said something that really stuck with me. He said, "If you do what you love, the money will find you." He was telling me that if I did what I loved to do, I could make a career out of it. That was the year I left the public school system and Mr. D Math was born.

Most people are told that they cannot do what they love, but he was saying the opposite. Not only that, but he was also saying that by loving what I do, the money would find me. I was at a crossroads in my teaching career because I knew I could be more than a classroom teacher in a public school. I thought I would have to give up on teaching entirely and find something new. It was shortly after that conversation with my engineering friend that I began writing my own courses and working with those first amazing homeschool families I still know to this day. Both my pivot from business to teaching, and my pivot from public school teaching to education business owner, moved me closer to discovering how I could combine everything I loved—teaching, performing, and creating—into a career. Today, I too love what I do.

Now, you might say, "Money is not important to me." Maybe it isn't, but what is important to you? If you're doing what you love, what's important to you will find you. When I started Mr. D Math, money was important to me because I wanted to take care of my family. I discovered that by doing what I loved to do anyway, the money did find me—and I'm now able to do what I love every day! Once I stopped splitting my time and started really focusing on doing what I loved, the opportunities naturally kept finding me.

I know there are many people out there who didn't start their careers doing what they loved. They likely moved from doing something they thought they were *supposed* to do to doing something that they loved to do over time. Unfortunately, this isn't the case for everyone.

The good news is that education today is changing. Young people are finally being asked what they love to do, and educators are listening. Young adults are thinking about their passions as they join the workforce. They're asked how they can turn doing what they love into a lifestyle *and* a career. If you're into gaming, get into the gaming industry. If you're an actor or performer like I am, get into the performance industry. Be willing to dream, be willing to dare, and find a way to do what you love to do.

You'll find that doing what you love will naturally open the right doors for you, if not always the expected ones. Does it take practice? Yes, it does. Are there going to be times when it doesn't look like it's going to work out? You bet. So what do you do? Well, you set goals!

GOALS

Goal-setting is not just about pursuing what you love—it's one of the most essential skills in developing an independently responsible learner. In *Think and Grow Rich*, Napoleon Hill wrote about the power of having a "definite purpose," a clear direction that gives you something to aim for. The same is true for students. When a young person sets a goal, whether it's mastering a lesson, improving a skill, or tackling a challenge, they're naming their purpose. That single act shifts how they think. They start looking for solutions instead of obstacles, taking initiative instead of waiting for someone to tell them what to do, and practicing persistence when things get difficult. These are the same qualities Hill identified as the foundation for all success, and they align perfectly with becoming an independently responsible learner. In fact, that is why I've included a bonus chapter on goal-setting at the end of this book. In that chapter, I'll walk you step-by-step through my personal 3-step goal-setting process, the same one I've used for years and have taught to students, parents, and teachers worldwide. You'll learn exactly how to set goals that inspire, guide, and support the independently responsible learner your student is becoming.

For now, let me tell you the number one way to achieve any goal: persistence. Don't quit. Keep going. Keep playing. Keep practicing. Keep trying. Keep looking. Keep discovering. It's that simple. To achieve any goal, you must make it your burning desire. It must become the thing that gets you up in the morning.

A burning desire doesn't have to feel dramatic. Sometimes it begins as a small spark of curiosity, something that interests you enough to explore further. But over time, that spark can grow into passion.

Students often struggle with this concept. They ask things like, "What if you're not sure what you love to do? What if you don't know what your 'thing' is?" That's completely normal, especially for young people. You're not supposed to have your entire life figured out when you're a teenager. Part of becoming independently responsible is learning how to explore different avenues, experimenting with different ways of being and doing, and discovering yourself along the way.

So how do you figure out what you love? You keep looking. You pay attention to the moments when you feel energized or inspired. You notice the activities that make time move quickly or where you lose yourself in flow because you're so absorbed in what you're doing. You notice the subjects that make you ask MORE questions, not fewer. You follow the pull of your curiosity, even if you don't yet know where it will lead. And you give yourself permission to try new things, many things, without expecting that every attempt will lead to success or a lifelong passion. You give yourself permission to be bad at something new!

When you explore in this way, something powerful happens. You stop worrying about what you think you *should* be doing and start recognizing the things in your life that feel meaningful. And once you find something you love—even a small part of it—you have something worth building a goal around. By doing what you love, or even moving toward it, you begin shaping a life that aligns with your strengths, values, and ultimately, your purpose. You're not just finding a passion—you're finding *yourself*.

Now, is it going to take a few tries to figure out? Almost certainly. Are you going to have to ask for support? Absolutely. Should you reach out to other people who are already doing what you love to do? Yes, you should. Ask them how they got started, what they enjoy most about what they do, and what challenges they've faced in getting there. These conversations give you real information and show you possible paths to success. The good news is that people who love what they do are usually excited to share their work with others.

There are many different paths to doing what you love. No matter your interests, there are almost always countless ways to get involved!

A 5-STEP PROCESS FOR DISCOVERING WHAT YOU LOVE

Here is a simple step-by-step process you can use to help you start discovering what you love in a practical and meaningful way.

Step 1: Make a List of the Top Five Things You Love to Do

This list doesn't have to be perfect, and it doesn't have to be tied to a future career. Just write down five things that bring you joy, interest, excitement, or curiosity.

Example:

- Playing video games
- Drawing characters
- Listening to music
- Playing basketball
- Solving puzzles

This is the starting point.

Step 2: Explore the Possibilities Within Each Item

Now take each item on your list and ask: "What are all the different ways this interest could show up in the real world?" This will open your mind to possibilities you may not have known existed.

Example 1: Gaming

Loving games doesn't mean you need to "be a gamer". You could explore:

- Game design
- Coding
- Animation
- Story writing
- Sound effects and music
- Game testing
- E-Sports commentary
- Content creation

There are dozens of ways to be part of something you enjoy!

Example 2: Music

You might love performing, but you could also explore:

- Songwriting
- Audio engineering
- Producing
- Mixing and mastering
- Instrument building
- Artist management
- Event planning

The music world is full of roles most people never see!

Example 3: Sports

There is much more to sports than just the athletes. You can explore:

- Coaching
- Physical therapy
- Sports broadcasting
- Data analysis
- Refereeing
- Sports photography or videography
- Event operations

Your passion has more doors than you think.

Step 3: Talk to Someone Who Is Doing Something You Like

This step is powerful. Ask questions like:

- What do you enjoy most about what you do?
- How did you get started?
- What skills helped you the most?
- What surprised you about this field?

Example:
A student interested in video editing might talk to a YouTuber or someone who edits videos for a local business. A student who loves drawing might talk to a graphic designer, animator, or art teacher. Talking to people in the field will allow you to gain a realistic perspective of what's possible—and it may even take you down roads you never expected to follow!

Step 4: Choose One Small Action You Can Do This Week

Don't worry about "finding your life's purpose" today. Just focus on the next step.

For example:

- If you love gaming, watch a video on how games are designed.
- If you love drawing, sketch one new character this week.
- If you love sports, practice a new skill or research coaching drills.
- If you love music, learn one new chord or watch a behind-the-scenes studio video.

These tiny actions will help you build momentum and keep you focused on your passion.

Step 5: Put One Thing You Love Into Your Daily Routine

Even 10 minutes a day matters. For example,

- Draw for 10 minutes.
- Read about a sports strategy.
- Play your instrument.
- Code a simple animation.
- Write in your journal.
- Watch a tutorial.

Doing something you love each day helps you understand yourself better, which is the foundation of becoming an independently responsible learner. When you make a list, explore possibilities, ask questions, and take daily action, you're not just figuring out what you love; you're training your brain to think, discover, and act. Those are the exact skills that shape goal-setting and lifelong learning. That is where passion and purpose meet.

DOING WHAT YOU LOVE IS A MODEL FOR YOUR CHILDREN

By doing these things every day, you're going to get very good at them. You're also going to start engaging more and more with the things you love to do. This changes how you present yourself to the world, and how the world sees you in turn. People will begin to see you for what you love to do. If you spend time drawing, people will see you as an artist. If you spend your free time writing, they will see you as a writer. If you spend your free time playing sports, people will come to see you as an athlete.

I've had students tell me that they don't know what they love, so I simply start by asking them what they did that day. They start to tell me, and the next thing they know, it's like a piece of popcorn in a pan! They discovered what it is they love to do just by looking at how they chose to spend their time.

TEACH

As parents, more than anything else, we want our children to be happy and successful in their lives. But it is important to recognize that our kids observe and model themselves after us to a certain extent. If you're a young person looking at your parents and notice that maybe they're not doing what they love, ask them what they actually love to do. Parents, if you're reading this, it's okay for you to do what you love to do because that gives your children permission to do the same. So don't hold back.

Chapter 10

MASTERMIND

This chapter is designed to give students a way to collaborate with other independently responsible learners. Masterminds allow groups of students to come together and support one another, through mutual accountability and coaching, on their journey to becoming more independent and responsible learners.

WHAT IS A MASTERMIND?

Simply put, a Mastermind is a group of two or more people working together in harmony toward a common goal. In bringing multiple people together, Masterminds create a level of thinking and power that is greater than the sum of its parts. Masterminding is a powerful tool for achieving your goals, and whether you're a student, a parent, or an educator, this chapter will guide you through how Masterminds work and how they can support your journey as an independently responsible learner.

Let's start with a key concept: synergy. Think of synergy like two minds coming together to create a third. The third mind is capable of producing more than either of the two minds could produce individually. That definition comes from an idea in Napoleon Hill's book *Think and Grow Rich*. When you participate in a Mastermind group, you bring multiple minds together in cooperation to create a "Master Mind."

A Mastermind group can be created by finding a cohort of people who are all interested in doing something meaningful with their lives. Sometimes, Masterminds are formed by bringing people together from different fields or interests. If you're a student, you can find peers who share your interests, even if you ultimately want to pursue different paths. Perhaps some students want to go to college, some want technical training, some may want to start a career right away, take a gap year, or join the military. Each of these students could be a valuable member of a Mastermind group.

Their varied perspectives will grant added insight to the Mastermind as a whole.

Ultimately, a Mastermind is a group of people with whom to share your interests and goals. The group doesn't have to consist of people that you already spend a lot of time with; you can even meet online.

To make a Mastermind of your own, you just need to find four other people to join you in it. Why do Masterminds have five people? Napoleon Hill never said "5 is the magic number," but if you study how effective Mastermind groups actually function, it seems that 4–6 people (with 5 as a sweet spot) is the ideal size. With five people, you get a decent range of perspectives, experiences, and problem-solving styles, without it feeling overcrowded. When first creating your Mastermind group, invite people who you think are up to something big in their lives. Let them know that you're creating a Mastermind group and you want them to be a part of it. You'll find that most people will agree because they're just as inspired to achieve their goals and dreams as you are!

Once you form your group, you should aim to meet once a week. Also, make sure you set an endpoint for the Mastermind. For example, you might agree to meet for six weeks, two months, six months, or even a year. It may seem odd, but Masterminds often work best when operating under a firm timeline. For your first Mastermind experience, I recommend setting a timeline of two months.

HOW TO RUN A MASTERMIND GROUP

Let's say, for example, your mastermind agrees to meet for the next two months. First, schedule a weekly meeting time. It's important to make sure that the schedule stays consistent. Typically, you'll want to meet for an hour each week. During your first meeting, each person should share what they want to accomplish during their time in the Mastermind group. For example, if you're committing to a two-month timeline, each member should lay out what they hope to accomplish over the next two months. Think of a goal you want to achieve through participating in the group. In subsequent meetings, members support each other in accomplishing the goals they set in the beginning. At the end of each session, every member commits to specific actions they will complete before the next meeting in order to move toward their goal. These promises are then reviewed, and new ones made, during the next meeting.

The promises you make to your Mastermind are intended to hold you accountable for moving toward your goals in a clear and measurable manner. They are meant to serve as smaller achievements to keep you moving toward your broader goal. When you make a promise to your Mastermind group, you're declaring what you will complete before the next meeting, choosing a deadline, and taking responsibility for following through. That's what gives the Mastermind its power: Your goals are strengthened by the accountability of the group, giving you the support you need to follow through.

So how do you run a Mastermind group? First, pick someone to be the leader—this is the moderator. The moderator keeps track of time, notes what people say, and records the promises they make to the group. Depending on how much responsibility they want to have, the moderator can do it all themselves, or they can assign tasks to other members. You may even want to consider being the moderator in order to expand your own leadership skills!

Over the course of each one-hour meeting, everyone gets 10 minutes to talk about what they've done since the last meeting. If they completed their promise, they describe what it was like to achieve that goal. If they did not meet their commitment, they reflect on what got in their way.

Finally, they can request any support they might need from others in the group. If someone runs out of time, the moderator can connect them with another member after the meeting is over to get additional support. Every 10 minutes, the focus switches to the next person until everyone has had a turn.

In a five-member Mastermind, that will account for 50 of the 60-minute session. During the last 10 minutes, there are two things the group needs to complete. First, the moderator reviews people's promises. This includes reviewing the promises that people made in the previous meeting, as well as new promises if appropriate. The second thing to complete is an acknowledgement party. The acknowledgement party is a time for each person to acknowledge or appreciate another member for something they shared during the meeting. It could be for a promise kept, or a courageous moment of vulnerability, or anything else. You might even appreciate someone for making a difference in your life through their sharing. If there is still time remaining, the moderator can then check to see if anybody left something out of their share. If more than an hour is necessary to achieve all of these points, it is OK to agree to lengthen meetings as a group. It is your Mastermind, so make it work for you!

In a Mastermind group, it's important that you don't share your opinions or interrupt others while they're talking. Let people speak during their 10 minutes. Listen to them as they talk about creating and reaching their goals. Taking notes is a great way to remember your own ideas without interrupting the speaker.

Often, in Masterminds, someone will share something that they're working on that will spark an idea for you that you'd never thought of before. That's the synergy. Two heads—or in this case, five heads—really are better than one! Come together, work together, Mastermind.

Be ready to show up to each meeting to talk about your successes *and* failures. And remember, the independently responsible learner isn't afraid of making mistakes. In every mistake or failure, there's a success waiting to happen. Failures lead to breakthroughs, and breakthroughs lead to miracles. And it can all start with a Mastermind.

KEEPING GOALS ALIVE

A Mastermind group is "completed" when the time frame you set at the beginning comes to an end. For example, if your group agreed to meet once a week for two months, you complete the Mastermind when those two months are over. At that point, everyone reflects on the goals they set, what they accomplished, what they learned, and how the group supported them. Completion simply means closing the agreed-upon cycle and acknowledging the progress made. After you complete one Mastermind group, you'll likely want to start the next one. They're that effective! You can continue with the same group or even start a brand-new Mastermind. You can continue with the members of your first group, or you may want to invite new people to join your group. You may even want to take on the role of a leader this time!

Ultimately, Masterminding is about creating synergy—that powerful third mind that only exists when multiple people come together with a shared purpose and burning desires. If you're a skeptic, then you should really try it! See if you can prove me wrong. If you're interested in discussing Masterminds in more detail or even joining one with me, go to **www.mrdfreeresources.com.**

At the core, Masterminds help their members reach their goals. But how do you set a goal in the first place? Remember what I said earlier: Don't quit! Stay in the game and keep going. You can make adjustments to your plan as you go, but the key is to just keep moving forward. The Mastermind group will give you a structure to keep your goals and dreams alive.

As you use Mastermind groups and surround yourself with people who support your growth, you'll notice something powerful: Goals become clearer, easier to track, and more achievable when you give them structure. That's exactly why I included a bonus section in this book to walk you through the goal-setting process. You'll learn how to break big dreams into manageable steps, how to stay accountable, and how to keep your goals alive from one week to the next. Think of it as a roadmap for turning your ideas and burning desires into real results.

Remember that independently responsible learning isn't about mastering any one method but about embodying the mindset of lifelong learning. The independently responsible student takes ownership of their education and learns to question everything, explore new ways of doing things, and bring these lessons into their everyday lives. All that matters is that you try—and be willing to learn along the way.

Bonus Chapter

GOAL-SETTING

REDEFINING GOALS

This chapter is my gift to you. I hope you will share it with many others. I hope you literally give this knowledge away! The more people who use goal-setting in this manner, the more people will realize their dreams. So, how do you get there?

We often ask young people what they want to be when they grow up. I've noticed that as children get older, they start to become more curious about opportunities and less definite about the answer to that question. When I ask a student, "What do you want to be when you grow up?" I get a response like this: "I don't know. I kind of like the idea of going into medicine. I kind of like the idea of being in law. I like the idea of engineering and tinkering with things with my hands. I like the idea of music." If you take any one of those topics, you'll notice that there is a whole world of possibilities inside each of them.

One of the best ways to support young people in figuring out what they want to do in their lives is to have them practice creating and achieving goals. The more young people (or anyone, for that matter) do this, the more they'll begin to discover the life they were born to live.

People say that good goals should be SMART: Specific, Measurable, Attainable, Relevant, and Timely. But I instead look to self-fulfilling prophecies. When I define a self-fulfilling prophecy, I start with the "self." The self is you. That's simple enough, right? But what is it to fulfill something? To fulfill something is to put it into effect. So self-fulfilling means that you're putting something into effect.

What is a prophecy? A prophecy is a prediction of something to come. Therefore, a self-fulfilling prophecy is the act of realizing the prediction of something to come. You get to say how things are going to go, then you get to make sure they happen. This is the philosophy of the independently responsible learner!

What you say makes a difference. You've probably heard that complaining about a bad situation makes it worse by focusing your attention on the negative. Similarly, expressing gratitude for the good aspects of your life makes it better by focusing your attention on the positive.

Have you ever woken up in the morning and decided, at that moment, that it was going to be a bad day? You probably ended up being right. Or have you lamented that an upcoming test wouldn't go well? You were probably right about that, too. I often say that people are constantly creating self-fulfilling prophecies. They're predicting how things are going to go, and those predictions make themselves come true. The independently responsible learner can use this dynamic for their own good.

Did you wake up this morning and look in the mirror? When you looked in the mirror, did you say to yourself, "Hello there, brilliant, talented, amazing, beautiful person?" Did you say, "Good morning, thank you for being me?" That's not how most people wake up in the morning. It can take practice to get good at speaking kindly of your own reflection. But what does it mean if something is not natural or normal to us? It just means that we need to keep training at it. In fact, it is not natural or normal to wake up in the morning and say, "Oh, you again," or "Today is going to be a terrible day," either. We learn that habit as well. So, how do you go about creating and fulfilling a better self-fulfilling prophecy? Let me give you three easy steps.

Step 1: Determine what you want.
Step 2: Determine when you're going to get it.
Step 3: Create the future.

STEP 1

I'm going to go through each step one at a time, with visuals. These visuals will help you start practicing your own goal-setting. Go to **www.mrdfreeresources.com** to download your free goal-setting diagrams for this chapter.

Start by writing down two sentences in your big rectangle. The first one is for you to write down what you want. The second is for your timeline, which should be one year, in this case. So whatever today's date is, add one year to it. Put that towards the bottom right-hand corner of your rectangle. That's your goal.

It can be anything with the exception that it cannot be about another person. At this point, some readers may be thinking that what they want more than anything is for their family to be happy. That's great! But if you want your family to be happy, you have to be happy first. This is about *you* and what *you* want for yourself and *your* life.

If you're a young person, maybe you're hoping to get into a college or get a new car. Maybe you just want to finally get around to cleaning your room. If you're a parent, perhaps you're building a new addition onto your house. Maybe you're taking that amazing vacation you've always wanted to take. Or maybe you want to earn more money. Whatever it is, make sure it inspires you.

I call this the cluster diagram.

STEP 2

Now look at the ovals in your visual. For each oval, think of one thing that you would need to do before what you wrote in your rectangle can happen. Let's look at buying a new car as an example.

Big rectangle: I will buy a new car by December 1, 2027.

The four ovals:
1. Research the kind of car I want to own.
2. Make a budget for buying the car.
3. Research expenses for owning a car.
4. Test drive cars.

Now, for each of the small eight rectangles in the visual, write down what you'll need to do to accomplish whatever sub-goal is recorded in their associated oval. Think of two things that have to happen to make the oval task achievable. All of the eight small rectangles and ovals are now working together to make the big rectangle goal a reality.

Big rectangle: I will buy a new car by December 1, 2027.

The four ovals:
1. Research the kind of car I want to own
2. Make a budget for buying the car
3. Research expenses for owning a car
4. Test drive cars

The two small rectangles:
1. Research the kind of car I want to own.
    Rectangle 1 - Ask 10 people what kind of car I should buy.
    Rectangle 2 - Go online and search for the best cars currently on the market, both new and used.

2. Make a budget for buying the car.
   Rectangle 1 - Determine the price of the car I want to buy based on what I can afford.
   Rectangle 2 - Figure out a 12-month plan for getting the money, including savings, gifts, or loans.

3. Research expenses for owning a car.
   Rectangle 1 - Go online and search for a list of expenses for owning a car.
   Rectangle 2 - Ask five people about the unexpected expenses they encountered once they owned a car.

4. Test drive cars
   Rectangle 1 - Test drive a new car.
   Rectangle 2 - Test drive a used car.

You have now created what I call a cluster diagram for your goal. This visual display is something that you can take with you and put in your notebook, car (if you already have one), bedroom, or bathroom. I highly recommend putting it on the bathroom mirror and reading it out loud to yourself every day when you wake up to remind yourself of your goal!

In our car example, the diagram would look like this:

So what have you done? You've created the action steps necessary to achieve your goal. You now need to make a timeline. Inside the ovals, specify the date by which each action should be completed. Maybe it's ongoing. So when do you start? Today? Next week? A month from now? If it'll be over a period of time, record both the start and the end dates on the diagram.

For the car example, you will want to know when to start and stop your savings. When and how many cars do you want to test drive? You may want to do your test drives over the course of a few months.

STEP 3

In Step 1, you specified your goal and figured out when you wanted to have achieved it by. In Step 2, you laid out intermediate goals to act as stepping stones along the way. Now, Step 3 is to create the reality you actually want. People often say that when you are out to create a future, you should begin with the end in mind. I couldn't agree more. Imagine you got in the car and pulled out of your driveway without knowing where you were going. Beginning with the end in mind makes for a much better journey *and* destination.

Step 3 is to write a reflective story as if you had already achieved your stated goal. In the story, you should reflect back on what happened that allowed you to achieve all the things you needed to do to reach your goal. In your mind, imagine that each step happened just the way you wanted it to.

To begin your story, start in the future. One year in the future, to be exact. Your story begins on the date your goal was (will be) achieved. First, describe how you feel after you've gotten what you wanted. Where are you? What are you wearing? What are you doing? How are you feeling? Who are you with? Trust your instincts.

From the future, go back and reminisce about all the things that happened along the way. Think about when they happened and how they got you to your desired outcome. Use everything you've written down in your ovals and small rectangles as reference points in your story. You start your story one year from now and then retrace all the way back to today, the day you created your goal.

Whatever you write down can—and often does—happen exactly the way you create it, that is the self-fulfilling prophecy. So this is your chance to have fun, to be creative, and open yourself to a world where anything is possible. Once you're done writing your story, read it aloud to yourself. Then, find five people with whom you can share your story. Usually, when I tell people to share their goals, they're afraid. But the reasons why they don't want to do it are the exact reasons why they should!

SHARING YOUR STORY

Most people hesitate to share their goals because doing so requires them to be vulnerable. The moment you speak a goal aloud, it becomes real. And that can be intimidating. People fear being judged for wanting something others might see as too big, too ambitious, or even too unrealistic. They worry about failing, and even more, about failing where others can see it. Sometimes they hold back because of past experiences where their dreams were dismissed or discouraged. And in many cases, people don't feel "ready" yet. They think they must already be the future version of themselves before declaring their desires for the future.

But these reasons, the fear of judgment, the fear of failure, and the fear of being seen trying, are the exact reasons you *should* share your goals. When you share a goal, you create accountability, clarity, and momentum. Sharing your goals invites support, encouragement, and the synergy that arises when others believe with you and walk alongside you. And when you read your story aloud to someone, you're not just telling them what you plan to do, you're setting your mind to it. You're speaking your future into existence. You create a self-fulfilling prophecy. That's the real power behind sharing your goals.

Once you share your future with someone else, the next time you're around that person, they will remember you as the future 'you' you created. They might also hold you accountable, helping you honor what you said you were going to do by asking about your goals when they see you. They naturally become your accountability partners. They'll have your back, and they'll want you to succeed.

I've been using this goal-setting process for over 30 years, and without fail, each year on January 1, I create my year. Believe me, it works. This is how you live with purpose and intention.

As we come to the end of our journey together, I would love to know your goals, dreams, and stories of becoming independently responsible learners with me. I invite you to reach out on my website or social media to share your experiences and contact us through **https://mrdmath.com/**! The journey of the independently responsible learner is lifelong, so I want to encourage you to keep going, even when it's hard. Believe in yourself, do what you love to do, and be extraordinary. Parents, keep believing in your learners. Students, keep believing in yourself. The world is ready for the independently responsible learner, and now, you're ready for the world.

A NOTE FROM ME TO YOU

Thank you for opening these pages and considering the ideas that led me to the independently responsible learner. It's been an honor to share these ideas—developed over years of teaching, coaching, and learning alongside my students—with you.

You've taken the time to reflect, ask questions, and explore what's possible. That puts you in rare company, because most people are content to spend their lives doing things the way they always have. Taking a step in a new direction makes you a pioneer.

As you continue supporting your independently responsible learners—or becoming one yourself—you'll likely encounter bumps along the road. These bumps will become learning opportunities if you're willing to change your relationship with mistakes and failure, as discussed in this book. The good news is that you're not alone on your journey. I'm here to support you when the path feels unclear, to help you reconnect with what's possible, and to celebrate every milestone, big or small, along the way. I am here for everyone, students, teachers, and parents alike.

If you ever need guidance, encouragement, or simply a reminder of why you started on this adventure in the first place, get in touch with me. Remembering why you're taking this on will also remind you of who you are: talented, amazing, and unstoppable. We're in this together, and I'm cheering you on every step of the way.

Here's to everything that's possible.

Mr. D.

ABOUT THE AUTHOR

Dennis DiNoia, M.A.Ed., known to families around the world as Mr. D, is an educator, speaker, curriculum creator, and pioneer in student-driven learning. With more than 35 years of experience working with young people, from struggling students in dropout-prevention programs to high-achieving homeschoolers, and every learner in between. He has dedicated his life to helping students develop one of the most essential skills for success: becoming independently responsible learners.

Mr. D began his career as a public school math teacher, where an unexpected experiment with self-grading transformed not only his classroom, but his entire philosophy of education. He discovered that when students check their own work, teach back what they've learned, and take ownership of their learning process, their confidence grows, their curiosity ignites, and mastery becomes possible for every student—not just a select few.

Today, Mr. D is the founder of Mr. D Math, a global online learning platform that has empowered tens of thousands of students to succeed in mathematics and beyond. His courses, workshops, and teaching methods emphasize independence, critical thinking, personal responsibility, and mastery through discovery. His approach has transformed families, inspired educators, and helped countless young people gain the confidence to direct their own learning. Visit **www.mrdfreeresources.com** to discover how Mr. D can help you.

As a professional educator with a Master's Degree in Education, Dennis has spoken at homeschool conferences across the country, trained parents and teachers, and mentored countless students who credit his methods with helping them thrive academically, personally, and professionally.

Beyond teaching, Mr. D is a lifelong learner, musician, performer, and creator who believes that discovering what you love and doing it with purpose is at the heart of a fulfilling life. His passion for helping young people uncover their strengths and step into their potential continues to drive everything he does.

Through this book, Mr. D invites parents, teachers, and students into the transformational journey he began decades ago: The move away from teacher-dependent educational models and toward student-led learning. A move that takes learning from an obligation to a source of confidence, ownership, and joy that leads to knowledge. To learn more about his work, book him for a speaking convention, or demo his courses, visit **mrdmath.com** or connect with him on his socials.

Mr. D was asked for a quote several years ago by a colleague who taught creative writing. He said, "Want new things, think new thoughts." He still lives by this quote today.

PRAISE FOR *TEACH*

TEACH is one of the most practical and encouraging homeschool books I've read! Dennis DiNoia breaks down the mindset and skills behind raising independently responsible learners in a way that truly makes sense. His strategies are simple to apply, work with any curriculum, and genuinely help kids take ownership of their learning. I walked away feeling equipped, inspired, and far more confident in how to guide my children toward a true love of learning. Every homeschool parent can benefit from the clarity and vision this book provides!

Sara Radginski - https://www.instagram.com/blessedhomeschoolblog/

TEACH gave me a fresh mindset and simple strategies for raising confident and independent learners. Mr.D's approach is clear, encouraging, and easy to put into practice.

Amy Milcic - rockyourhomeschool.net

As a homeschool mom and former educator, learning the nuances of teaching from an expert in his field is invaluable. This is a resource that reinvigorates and nourishes the latent teacher in all of us.

Christal Gamble - https://www.instagram.com/mamasweetbaby/

PRAISE FOR *TEACH*

TEACH by Dennis DiNoia will reshape how you think about learning. This book is a refreshing, conversational guide that makes empowering our children to become confident, self-directed learners feel achievable—not overwhelming. Dennis's insights on asking meaningful questions, encouraging responsibility, and teaching with purpose have given me so many practical ideas I can implement right away. Whether you're a parent, educator, or teen, this book offers encouragement and tools to cultivate a lifelong love of learning.

Sara Jordan - https://heartandsoulhomeschooling.com

TEACH: Creating Independently Responsible Learners is more than a book about education. It constitutes a mindset shift for parents and students alike. Dennis DiNoia has the rare ability to make learning feel both practical and empowering, moving far beyond checklists, grades, and rigid systems. His focus on helping children learn how to think, take ownership of their work, and connect learning to what they love is exactly what so many families are searching for. Written with warmth, clarity, and real-life wisdom, *TEACH* equips parents to step into the role of coach and gives students the confidence to become independently responsible learners. It is a must-read for homeschool families and anyone who wants education to truly prepare children for life.

Shawna Wingert - https://differentbydesignlearning.com/

Mr. D provides a compelling account of how he crafted his unique teaching philosophy. Through his years as a public school teacher, he experimented with various methodologies and discovered that student engagement soared when learners were empowered to identify their own mistakes and make meaningful corrections. This approach fosters a strong sense of accountability and ownership over learning. He also emphasizes the value of having students teach back what they've learned to a parent or guardian, a process that not only reinforces mastery of the subject but also sharpens communication and presentation skills. Ultimately, the lessons learned in his math classes extend far beyond the classroom, equipping students to become independent, self-motivated individuals who take pride in their work.

Having used Mr. D's philosophy firsthand, I can personally attest to its lasting impact. I was amazed to watch my daughter apply these principles not only in math, but in all areas of her life. After receiving a D on her first Chemistry exam at our local co-op, she didn't feel defeated or discouraged. Instead, she approached her chemistry teacher and asked if she could review her mistakes, correct them, and retake the exam for a better grade. Her teacher—who had over 25 years of experience—was stunned and said, "In all my years of teaching, I have never had a student ask me that." She was genuinely thrilled to see a student so invested in her own learning and gladly provided the opportunity for her to grow and succeed.

To this day, I still see my daughter apply what she learned through Mr. D's math approach to improve not only her academic performance, but also her character and work ethic. The confidence, accountability, and perseverance she developed as an independently responsible learner are skills that will serve her for a lifetime.

Lourdes Michael - Homeschool mom of 3

www.ingramcontent.com/pod-product-compliance
Lightning Source LLC
LaVergne TN
LVHW010948110826
845149LV00015B/3259

* 9 7 8 1 9 5 6 8 3 7 8 4 1 *